Advance Praise for S

With so much research tying social me
depression, anxiety, and addiction, it's never been a better time for a guided journey to unplug. In *Social Media Reset*, Allie Marie Smith takes you by the hand on a thirty-day program that will boost your mood, calm your stress, and enhance your life. And what a beautiful life it can be when you aren't tethered to your devices.

DANIEL G. AMEN, MD Author of *Change Your Brain, Change Your Life*

Allie Marie Smith has the voice of a wise guide, a relatable writer, and a compassionate friend. Her newest book is more than a rest from social media; it's also a reset for your soul that will help you realign with what matters most to you. Allie offers spiritual truth, mental health insights, practical strategies, and more in this little book that's sure to have a big impact on your life!

HOLLEY GERTH *Wall Street Journal* bestselling author of *You're Already Amazing* and *The Powerful Purpose of Introverts*

This book is such a radical joy journey! It should be annual required reading for every woman of every age who participates in social media. As a personal friend (and an adventure partner) of Allie's, I see firsthand the beauty of someone who puts social media in its place. Each chapter is relatable and filled with truth, and will make you want to run hard after good and beautiful things. Get this into the hands of every girl in your life who uses social media!

KATE MERRICK Author of *And Still She Laughs* and *Here, Now*

Did you know that if you spend a handful of hours on social media every day, it can add up to fifteen years of your life? It's time for a reset. You don't have to fill your time with constant scrolling and comparison. Start this journey with Allie instead. There's so much more God has for your life!

ARLENE PELLICANE Author of *Calm, Cool, and Connected* and host of the *Happy Home Podcast*

This book is a necessary wake-up call to silence the relentless noise of our screens and lean into the still, sacred presence of the Father. With tender wisdom, Allie unveils a vision for a life brimming with true peace, joy, and connection—not found in the glow of a screen but in the radiance of God's love. For anyone longing to break free from digital distraction and cultivate a deeper, more vibrant intimacy with the Lord, *Social Media Reset* is a beautiful road map to renewal and reconnection.

BRITTANY MAHER Two-time bestselling author and founder of Her True Worth

Allie offers the honest yet compassionate guidance we all need to put down our phones and wake up to the beauty of life happening around us. *Social Media Reset* is timely, practical, and transformative. Do your soul a favor by reading this book and putting it into practice. You'll be so glad you did.

ROBIN LONG Founder of Lindywell and author of *Well to the Core*

We have all heard about the mental, emotional, and relational costs of social media. But what do we do? Allie is both an inspiration and a guide as she teaches us how to not simply *think* about change but *practice* the change we long to experience around social media! If you're looking for a resource that's rooted in wisdom and offers practical steps toward lasting growth, look no further. After reading this book, I can confidently say that this is a book we all need *and* want!

NICOLE ZASOWSKI Marriage and family therapist and author of *What If It's Wonderful?*

What Readers Are Saying

I'd known for a while that I was using social media to numb out, and I'd tried deleting these apps from my phone and taking breaks, but nothing changed . . . until this book. Each short chapter gently exposed the roots of my unhealthy relationship with social media, equipped me with a grace-filled perspective, and left me feeling refreshed and connected to God. This is the reset I was waiting for.
JENNA SPRADLEY

Before reading *Social Media Reset*, I found myself "quickly" checking social media all throughout the day. While reading Allie's book, I was convicted to examine my heart. I still have social media, but I've set healthy boundaries and I no longer have the desire to check it like I once did.
CHERI HULST

As a new, expectant mother, I was feeling extremely overwhelmed by the Instagram algorithms showing me what all new mothers "have to" have or do before baby comes. This book challenged me to really think about why and how I use social media, and how I can approach it differently moving forward. *Social Media Reset* offers a great mix of biblical truths and practical tips to help women in all life stages discern how they want to interact with social media and how else they can spend their time in a way that's aligned with purpose and value.
MOLLY HAYES

Reading this book and taking a break from social media was not just a reset—it was a transformative journey. Each day, I was invited to embrace a full and rich life, free from the distraction of social media, and rediscover my joy in a way I never thought possible.
BONNIE NICHOLS

In *Social Media Reset*, Allie shares her personal experiences and useful tips for taking a break from social media. This book paints a new and exciting picture of what a flourishing life can look like. As you embark on your own thirty-day social media reset, Allie will challenge you to pray more, reflect honestly, and live out truths from the Bible. This is a reset you don't want to miss!

DANIELLE CEKANOR

SOCIAL MEDIA RESET

SOCIAL MEDIA RESET

A 30-Day Guided Journey to Unplug, Reconnect with God, and Reclaim Your Joy

ALLIE MARIE SMITH

TYNDALE REFRESH®

Think Well. Live Well. Be Well.

Visit Tyndale online at tyndale.com.

Visit the author online at alliemariesmith.com.

Tyndale, Tyndale's quill logo, *Tyndale Refresh*, and the Tyndale Refresh logo are registered trademarks of Tyndale House Ministries. Tyndale Refresh is a nonfiction imprint of Tyndale House Publishers, Carol Stream, Illinois.

Social Media Reset: A 30-Day Guided Journey to Unplug, Reconnect with God, and Reclaim Your Joy

Copyright © 2025 by Allie Marie Smith. All rights reserved.

Cover and interior photograph of watercolor abstract copyright © Liliia/Adobe Stock. All rights reserved.

Author photo by Lena Britt Ibarra, copyright © 2024. All rights reserved.

Designed by Eva M. Winters

Edited by Stephanie Rische and Claire Lloyd

Published in association with the literary agency, WTA Media LLC, Franklin, TN.

All Scripture quotations, unless otherwise indicated, are taken from the Holy Bible, *New International Version*,® *NIV*.® Copyright © 1973, 1978, 1984, 2011 by Biblica, Inc.® Used by permission. All rights reserved worldwide.

Scripture quotations marked ESV are from The ESV® Bible (The Holy Bible, English Standard Version®), copyright © 2001 by Crossway, a publishing ministry of Good News Publishers. Used by permission. All rights reserved.

Scripture quotations marked KJV are taken from the *Holy Bible*, King James Version.

Scripture quotations marked MSG are taken from *The Message*, copyright © 1993, 2002, 2018 by Eugene H. Peterson. Used by permission of NavPress. All rights reserved. Represented by Tyndale House Publishers.

Scripture quotations marked NASB are taken from the (NASB®) New American Standard Bible,® copyright © 1960, 1971, 1977, 1995, 2020 by The Lockman Foundation. Used by permission. (Some quotations may be from the earlier NASB edition, copyright © 1995.) All rights reserved. www.lockman.org.

Scripture quotations marked NKJV are taken from the New King James Version,® copyright © 1982 by Thomas Nelson. Used by permission. All rights reserved.

Scripture quotations marked NLT are taken from the *Holy Bible*, New Living Translation, copyright © 1996, 2004, 2015 by Tyndale House Foundation. Used by permission of Tyndale House Publishers, Carol Stream, Illinois 60188. All rights reserved.

The URLs in this book were verified prior to publication. The publisher is not responsible for content in the links, links that have expired, or websites that have changed ownership after that time.

For information about special discounts for bulk purchases, please contact Tyndale House Publishers at csresponse@tyndale.com, or call 1-855-277-9400.

ISBN 979-8-4005-0804-2

Printed in the United States of America

31	30	29	28	27	26	25
7	6	5	4	3	2	1

To Paul, my surf cowboy.
Thanks for a life of laughter, adventure, and joy.
Here's to forever.

Contents

INTRODUCTION: Is It Time for a Reset? *1*
DAY 1: Restoring Your Soul *17*
DAY 2: Your Wild and Precious Life *21*
DAY 3: Wonderfully Made *25*
DAY 4: The Truest Thing about You *29*
DAY 5: Coming Home *34*
DAY 6: Be the Decorator of Your Life *38*
DAY 7: Pulling Weeds *42*
DAY 8: The Beauty of an Unseen Life *46*
DAY 9: The Strength of Solitude and Silence *50*
DAY 10: A Heart at Rest *54*
DAY 11: Looking for Likes, Longing for Love *59*
DAY 12: Lady Wisdom and Lady Folly *63*
DAY 13: A Healthy Brain and a Sound Mind *67*
DAY 14: Showing Up as Your True Self *72*
DAY 15: You Are Not an Imposter *77*
DAY 16: Breaking Up with Your Ideal Self *81*
DAY 17: Grieving Broken Dreams *85*
DAY 18: All the Feelings *89*
DAY 19: Healing from Shame *93*
DAY 20: Finding Your People *97*

DAY 21: Beauty Secrets *102*
DAY 22: Making Peace with Your Body *106*
DAY 23: How to Live Happier and Healthier *110*
DAY 24: The Mean Sisters *114*
DAY 25: Defining Success *119*
DAY 26: Freedom and Grit *124*
DAY 27: How to Really Change Your Life *128*
DAY 28: Whimsy, Rest, Wonder, and Play *133*
DAY 29: A Glorious Adventure *138*
DAY 30: Live Fully, Wholly Alive *142*

After the Reset *147*

APPENDIX 1: 75 Things You Can Do Instead of Scrolling on Social Media *151*
APPENDIX 2: Social Media Quiz *155*
APPENDIX 3: Social Media Formula *157*
APPENDIX 4: Ideas for Social Media Boundaries *159*
APPENDIX 5: More Reflection Questions *163*
APPENDIX 6: Well-Being Assessment Inventory *167*
APPENDIX 7: Father's Love Letter *173*
APPENDIX 8: Prayer to Give Your Life to God *179*
Acknowledgments *181*
Notes *183*
About the Author *189*

INTRODUCTION

Is It Time for a Reset?

Joy does not simply happen to us. We have to choose joy and keep choosing it every day.
HENRI J. M. NOUWEN

The golden California sun kissed my face as I paddled through salty water on my ten-foot single-fin longboard. Dolphins danced in the distance, showing off with aerial twists and tricks. In a colony of six, brown pelicans gracefully glided three feet above the water, waiting for the right moment to completely submerge themselves and scoop up dozens of sardines for breakfast. I was enveloped by the beauty of our Santa Barbara coast, but rather than soaking in the splendor of it all, I was distracted and restless. My thoughts turned to another place—a pixelated, virtual world called social media. The refuge and peace the sea usually brought me were stolen by the chaos of a digital world I wasn't even in. Ironically, here I was in a perfect "Instagrammable" moment when the last thing I should be doing was thinking about Instagram, obsessing about Instagram. I was in a mental tug-of-war: part of me couldn't resist the pull of social media, and part of me wanted to quit altogether.

I should go off social media forever. But I'll miss out on so much, and I want to keep in touch with friends. I need to be on it for work and to grow my following if I want to publish another book. I should probably start making reels—they get a lot more views than just posts. Why doesn't she follow me back? I can't believe they didn't invite me to the rodeo. I want to buy that pair of cognac leather boots I saw in that ad. I can't believe I posted that selfie. People probably think I'm self-absorbed. But everyone posts selfies. No, I should take it down.

I appreciated how social media allowed me to reconnect with old friends and stay in touch with people. I enjoyed posting photos and sharing updates. But over time, as the features and algorithms changed and I continued to overuse it, I began to hate the way social media made me feel. It left me with feelings of inadequacy, making me discontent and self-conscious. It became a means through which I searched for connection and human approval but never found it. The comparisons it brought out made me fail to see the beauty and wonder in my life and kept me from being fully present with the people I love most.

With every uninteresting moment or lull in my day, my thumb would instinctively tap my apps in search of an addictive dopamine hit caused by the notification of a new like, comment, or friend request. I would compulsively toggle between all my social media apps and refresh my screen in search of another hit. I would often fall asleep to the endless scrolling of photographs posted by friends and strangers. If I woke up in the middle of the night unable to fall back asleep, I would hide my phone under the covers and turn onto my side away from my husband to not wake him while I scrolled until the drum of thousands of pixels rocked me back to sleep. The next morning, I would wake up, immediately reach for my phone, and open the apps to see what I had missed while the world was sleeping, and the cycle would start over again.

I knew something needed to change, but I didn't want to go off social media completely. I tried to create a healthier relationship with it. I would delete the app immediately after I posted a photo and caption so I wasn't tempted to obsessively check and recheck my posts to see if anyone had liked or commented on them. Then, I would redownload it from the app store the next time I wanted to post another photo. It went like this: Post. Delete. Redownload. Post. Delete. Redownload.

I give you this glimpse into what my relationship with social media became to reassure you that you're not alone if you can relate. It's a common experience, but be encouraged, friend—this reset will help you break free from the obsession with social media and help you enjoy a better life.

As an introvert who thrives on having a peace-filled life, I think I am especially sensitive to the effects social media has on my mental well-being. The noise and chaos that come with it give my spirit a sense of angst and heightened anxiety. Even with the positive content I look at, I can often feel worse about myself and my life after using it. But when I'm unplugged and fully present in my life and the people and things I love, my spirit is at rest. I feel peaceful, grateful, and calm.

Over the past several years, I've set boundaries for myself that allow me to use social media in a way that mostly adds value to my life. I master it; it doesn't master me. Because I've really struggled with my mental health in the past, I do everything I possibly can to safeguard it. This is the number one reason behind my decision to minimally use social media. I also decided that being engrossed with and envious of others' lives is an insult to the God who gave me mine. I no longer fear missing out on what everyone else is doing, but I fear missing out on my own life. I'm also very intentional in my purpose for using social media. I enjoy using it to encourage others, keep up with friends, talk about my work, and share special moments of my life. Knowing my purpose for social media helps me avoid using it mindlessly.

I want to live digitally disconnected so I can be spiritually connected to God and my life. In addition to protecting my mental health, I believe using social media minimally will help me live a more productive life, accomplish my goals, and have deep relationships. Detaching from my phone helps me enjoy my life so much more—and makes me so much happier.

Even though I have overcome my social media addiction, I haven't arrived and still wrestle with it at times. There are many benefits to using social media, and it can add a lot of value to your life, which is why stepping away from it even for a little bit can be so difficult. But I promise that this thirty-day reset will improve your life. This journey will empower you to cultivate a more flourishing life, and at the end of your reset, you will be inspired to implement your own boundaries with social media to help you thrive. I will share many options for boundaries in the back of the book that you can choose for yourself. By the end of this thirty-day experience, you will be empowered to take control of your technology and live a full, abundant life. Your best life is waiting for you off your phone, and this guided journey will help you find it.

How Did We Get Here?

While social media offers us the revolutionary ability to connect with anyone in the world virtually, it is questionable if these platforms have deepened our sense of true community and brought humanity closer together. We are hyperconnected but emotionally disconnected and isolated. We are digitally connected but more polarized than ever. It is possible that humanity has never been more anxious, afraid, divided, depressed, suicidal, and lonely.

The constant flow of notifications, likes, follows, and messages from social media give our brains hits of dopamine and cause the same kind of chemical reaction seen with food, gambling, and drugs. Through these dopamine hits and the infinite scroll, our phones have become like handheld slot machines. The thing about dopamine is that it doesn't last long, so it's easy to get addicted to finding it. Eventually, the dopamine hit you get over time lessens, which makes you want to use social media even more to get the same amount of pleasure. Before you know it, this dopamine-induced loop catapults you into an unhealthy dependency on it, and your happiness and quality of life suffer.[1]

One of the most damaging components of social media for women is the chronic social comparisons it prompts. Comparison is a core part of human psychology that causes us to evaluate others, ourselves, and our external environment and circumstances. Comparison can inspire and motivate us to improve ourselves, but it can also give us a false bar for determining how we measure up, leading to either pride or insecurity and low self-worth.

Before the onset of modern media, we could only compare ourselves to people we knew in real life. But today, we can compare ourselves to the world's richest, most famous, and most beautiful people. Doing so lowers our self-worth, causes insecurity, and makes us feel discontent with our lives. While there is a trend to share more authentic content, the overall nature of social media is for it to be a highlight reel and showcase only the best parts, which never reflects reality. We compare ourselves not only to celebrities and influencers but to friends and acquaintances—and specifically, to the highly curated aspects of their lives. These well-known, timeless words stand true: "Comparison is the thief of joy."

A Destructive Toll

We are experiencing an unprecedented and preventable, technologically induced mental health crisis. The onset of social media has coincided with steep increases in anxiety, depression, self-harm, and suicide among young users, especially girls.[2]

Social media users access an average of 6.7 accounts a month and spend about two hours and twenty minutes daily on social media platforms.[3] Thirty-nine percent of US online users admit to feeling the addictive pull of the digital rabbit hole that is social media, with 9 percent of these users agreeing completely with the statement "I am addicted to social media." It appears a sizable proportion of users find the dopamine-fueled allure of social media difficult to resist.[4]

Teen girls spend more time on social media than adults and use it for an average of 5.3 hours a day, with many girls spending up to seven to nine hours on it daily.[5] Including social media usage, teenage girls spend an average of approximately eight hours and two minutes on a screen.[6] Given the clear evidence that excessive social media use worsens mental health, this means that girls and women can experience unnecessary mental health issues throughout their lives as a direct result of using social media.

While it can be harmful, social media in and of itself is not bad. It has no morality. It's about how you use it, what you look at and share, and how much time you spend on it. Social media can be used for a tremendous amount of good. It can be fun and add value to your life if you use it intentionally, with wisdom. It can be used to build relationships, start a business, share God's love and hope with other people, bring attention to causes you care about, allow you to express yourself creatively, and make others feel important and less alone. It can add value to your life and even make you a better person if you use it carefully and with intentionality.

You might find a lot of joy and fun in using social media, but overuse and comparison will hurt your well-being and rob you of a fulfilling life. Given its upsides and downsides, you can decide what kind of relationship you want with it—if any—and how you would like to show up on it. You can use it in a way that brings you joy and brightens other people's lives, and then you can happily ditch all the junk that comes with it. This social media reset will help you break any dependence you may have on it, reset your brain's pathways, and help you gain perspective on its influence on your life. These next thirty days will give you time to step away from your screen, refresh your soul, and recover your life.

Do You Need a Refresh?

There are social media users, and there are people with an unhealthy addiction to social media, which is the group I used to be in. I knew social media had become a problem when it became hard to go without it, began to decrease my happiness, and became something I thought about obsessively throughout my day. What motivated me to cut back on my social media usage was thinking about how much time over the course of my life I would spend on it instead of doing more important things.

Before we get too far in this book, it will be helpful to get some perspective on your use of technology and social media by doing a

IS IT TIME FOR A RESET?

brief inventory. Grab your phone, go to its settings, and locate where you can check your screen time and app usage (if your phone has this feature).

Write down your average daily phone usage over the past week.

_____

Write down the highest number of phone pickups or unlocks you have had over the past week.

_____

Now, look at all your app usage and website activity. Write down the social media accounts you use, and next to each one, list the average daily time you spent on them during the last week.

SOCIAL MEDIA	TIME SPENT
1.	
2.	
3.	
4.	
5.	
6.	
7.	
8.	
9.	
10.	

Add up the average daily time you have been spending on social media.

_____

SOCIAL MEDIA RESET

Now multiply this number by thirty and write it down. This totals the extra free time you will have in the next thirty days.

Now, to figure out how many years you are on track to spend on social media until you turn eighty (the average lifespan of a woman), complete the formula on page 157, taking into account your daily average use. Or look at the estimates provided below (based on someone who began using social media at thirteen).

Keep track of how many hours you use social media in an average day. Write your answer here:

If you use social media for one hour a day, you will end up spending roughly three years of your life on social media.

If you use social media for two to three hours a day, you will end up spending roughly six to eight years of your life on social media.

If you use social media for four or more hours a day, you will end up spending roughly eleven or more years of your life on social media.

Write down other apps or websites you frequently visit and list the time you have recently spent on each one.

Apps/Usage:

IS IT TIME FOR A RESET?

Write down your goals for your phone usage over the next thirty days, which will not include time on social media (since you will not be on it).

Goals:

_____

_____

_____

_____

_____

_____

_____

Total phone usage:

_____

Number of pickups or unlocks:

_____

Time spent on non–social media apps and websites:

_____

If you have a phone and social media addiction, this reset is going to be hard, but I know you can do hard things, and this time away can change your life. It will be worth it, and you won't regret it. Be warned that you might experience withdrawal. For several days or even weeks, you will probably find yourself instinctively reaching for your phone and tapping the screen to access your accounts. You might feel restless or irritable when you can't access them. You might find yourself experiencing uncomfortable feelings such as boredom, sadness, and anxiety, which social media has temporarily soothed in the past. This is normal and to be expected, so don't be hard on yourself. Learn to sit with these emotions and deal with them in healthy ways. As your reset unfolds, you will experience a new sense of freedom and calm.

Here are some tips to set you up for success. First, ensure you have your username and password for all of your social media accounts. Then, delete the apps from your phone and other devices (you can redownload them after this reset). If you are tempted to access them, ask a trusted friend or family member to change your password. After thirty days, you can redownload the apps. Do everything you can to make it impossible to access your accounts. If you slip and check your social media, have grace with yourself and start again. Just do the best you can.

Consider putting the Bible app where your social media accounts used to be so you begin to tap it instead. When you have the compulsion to check your accounts, call a friend, go on a walk, journal, or do something fun for yourself. Every time you do something else that's more positive and life-giving, your happiness muscles will be strengthened, and you will have more joy.

Set yourself up for success by doing this thirty-day life-changing experience with as many friends as possible. Pause here and text them right now to invite them to join you. This will give you accountability and create space to cultivate memories and meaningful face-to-face relationships. Get together for dinner, grab a coffee, go on walks, and have memorable experiences together that foster a genuine community you won't find online.

Avoid the temptation to swap out the time you've been spending on social media for other types of media, which will likely also negatively affect your well-being and distract you from this transforming experience. These types of media can include gaming websites, YouTube and other video streaming and photo-sharing sites like Pinterest, games on your phone, and excess TV shows and movies.

I recognize that many people rely on social media to support their businesses and careers. If you believe it is necessary to be on it for professional reasons, you can still choose to take a break from using it for personal and non-professional purposes. But to get the absolute most out of this life-changing experience, you'll want to take thirty days away and stop using it cold turkey.

The goal is to spend as little time on your phone and all media as possible and spend the time you get back doing more restorative activities offline that improve your well-being and cultivate true community. This would be an awesome time to try new things like baking sourdough bread, taking up a new hobby, writing poetry, playing a new instrument, volunteering, or doing something life-giving to fill up all the hours you'll get back. Think about the people, things, hobbies, and activities that bring you the most joy, and fill your extra time enjoying these.

Since phone and social media use involve the excessive movement of our fingers and hands, think about some tactile things you can do to keep them busy constructively. For example, maybe try watercolor, crocheting, or jewelry making, or consider writing letters to your friends and loved ones. I think you will find doing and creating things with your hands is more fulfilling than mindlessly scrolling on your phone.

Take an audit of your life. What can stay? What needs to go? See if there is anything else that will set you up for success in these next thirty days. If you pour your heart into this journey and ditch as many bad habits, hang-ups, negative relationships, and distractions as possible, it will be a transformative experience of personal growth that will change your life forever.

Craving Something Deeper

You are made for so much more than the empty life the world offers. The world of social media isn't where we were designed to live. Our fingers were not made to swipe a pixelated screen and watch other people's lives unfold. They were made for planting flowers in the dirt, making a meal for a hurting friend, combing through a child's hair, pointing at shooting stars, collecting seashells, creating art, thumbing through the pages of a book, helping those in need, working hard, and holding the hands of those you love. Your best life will never be found on your phone. We are so far removed from the life we've been created for, and it's making us sick.

We might think the mental health crisis today is only a result of social media, but that's just part of the story. Something deeper and more profound is happening. As we've become fixated on our phones, we've forgotten God. We have lost our way spiritually. God has been pushed out of our world, and we are suffering because of it.

More of ourselves and less of God is not working for us. As we have turned away from God, we have turned inward and to social media, where too often we have found emptiness and despair. We have failed to find answers to the fundamental questions of life, such as why we are here and the purpose of our lives. This has led to an identity crisis and a failed search for meaning. But as we return to God and find our identity, worth, and purpose in Him, we come alive. We discover our purpose; we find true connection; we cultivate hope; we overcome fear and build lives we love. Getting off social media will likely make you happier, but it won't fundamentally change your life. Only God can do that.

A Journey toward a Flourishing Life

I need to be honest with you. Some of what I share will be hard to hear. I'll be giving you some tough love. I only do this because I care about you and because I have experienced the joy and freedom that's found on the other side, and I want you to be able to do the same. I know firsthand that social media can be a real soul killer, and I want you to be happy and have the most amazing life possible. You are capable of more than you know, and you can do this reset even though it might be hard and countercultural.

This book is my attempt to inspire you to wake up to the gift of your life and live it to the fullest without any regrets. More than a social media reset, this book is a guide to living a really good life. I want you to get excited about your life and build a life you love. I want you to have the best life you can, but you can't have it if you're addicted to your phone. This experience is about falling asleep to comparison and digital distractions so you can live wide awake to the beauty of your precious and fleeting life. It's a dare to disappear on social media for thirty days and be mysterious online so you can live wide awake offline. It's an opportunity to disentangle yourself from the digital world and walk on a path toward a life overflowing with goodness, joy, and beauty.

Through my experience coaching women, I have found that we can only make limited progress on our journey toward spiritual and personal growth while we overuse social media. But when we take a break from it, wholeheartedly invest in our lives and relationship with God, and commit ourselves to personal growth, our breakthroughs are remarkable. As you wholeheartedly commit yourself to this journey, I believe you can experience tremendous transformation that will enrich your life.

Whatever your beliefs are about God, faith, spirituality, or Jesus, I hope you will join me with an open heart and mind. I hope you will leave this experience a different woman—one who is more alive and full of joy than she was before. To do so, I am sharing the truth and wisdom I have learned from the bestselling and most life-changing book in human history—the Bible.

God saved me from the pit of depression and brought me into His marvelous light. After hitting rock bottom as a young woman, I was transformed by the perfect love of Jesus, and I've been imperfectly following Him ever since. I see every second of my life as sacred, which is why I'm so serious about this social media thing.

Because of this, I can't just give you fluffy, feel-good words of my own making without sharing God's radical love and purpose for you. The principles, ideas, and wisdom I share are from this timeless instruction manual for human flourishing. I know the Bible can be intimidating and overwhelming, but I really think you'll find the words I share from it life-giving. Even if you're not interested in faith or spiritual things, you'll still get life-changing wisdom. If you want to learn more about God and my personal story, you can read my book *Wonderfully Made: Discover the Identity, Love, and Worth You Were Created For*.

In addition to a spiritual journey, this is a life-coaching experience without costing thousands of dollars. As a certified life coach and mentor to hundreds of girls and women, I will share principles and practical ideas that will propel you to your full potential and allow you to experience unprecedented breakthroughs. This wisdom has allowed me to go from a girl who didn't want to live anymore to a woman who can't wait to get out of bed.

How to Use This Book

I know the thought of going off social media for thirty days might be daunting, but just take it one day at a time. If you miss a day, no worries—just pick up where you left off. Each day, I will discuss a different topic and share principles to help you flourish in that area of your life. If possible, try to read in the morning so you can spend the rest of your day reflecting on that day's content. Plan a set-aside time and consider making a designated space to read, pray, and reflect. Grab a pen and take all the time you need to answer the reflection questions. Think about how you can make this experience fun. Maybe cozy up in your favorite quiet place with your favorite morning drink in your favorite mug. Light a candle, listen to your favorite playlist, or do whatever you can to make it as enjoyable of an experience as possible. As I mentioned earlier, I recommend you do this reset with friends so you can keep one another accountable and enjoy your reset together.

In the first appendix, there is a list of 75 things you can do instead of using technology, so if you find yourself unsure how to replace your phone habit, turn there throughout this reset! Also in the back of the book you will find a social media quiz to help you gauge what kind of impact social media is having on you. You will also be able to use a formula to determine how many days and years of your life you are on track to spend on social media, given your current average usage. These exercises can give you a fuller picture of social media's impact on your life and well-being. There is also a well-being assessment that will help you get an idea of how you are doing mentally, spiritually, and physically. I encourage you to complete this well-being assessment before day 1 and after day 30.

I also include a list of several ideas for social media boundaries. You can decide which boundaries to implement moving forward if you want to continue using social media. Lastly, there are additional reflection questions you can answer. I encourage you to take advantage of this content to get the most out of your journey.

A Brave Decision and a Better Life

You'll never find what you're really looking for on your phone. A better life awaits you if you don't conform to the social media circus. On the other side of this journey is your best life. It will never be an easy life free of hardship and suffering, but it will be a life worth living. Peace, joy, and contentment are yours for the taking as you throw yourself into this experience and lean into this journey of returning to God and reclaiming your joy. It's time to say goodbye to the emptiness and disappointments of social media and say hello to the better things of life. If you do this journey wholeheartedly, draw near to God, and begin to live out the principles in this book, your life won't be the same after these next thirty days.

Joy is a courageous decision to choose the kind of life you want to live. This decision empowers you to pursue the abundant life you were made for. Choosing joy requires hard work and sacrifices. If you want to have joy like no one else, you have to live like no one else. Joy is not something that will find you; it is a treasure you must search for daily. You must fight for it from sunrise to sunset. The fact that you picked up this book and are embarking on this journey to change your life shows that you are brave and can do hard things.

This journey is about unfollowing the world and following the ways of God, which leads to a flourishing life. This is your chance to reset your life and recover it—or truly find it for the first time. This is a chance to discover the identity and the purpose you've been created for. It's a call to return to God, yourself, and the people and things you love. I'm so glad you are here, and I hope every word will help you discover how loved and valuable you are and the amazing life you've been created for. Are you ready for a reset and a new beginning? Are you ready to get your life back? Your joy? Let's go, friend.

DAY 1

RESTORING YOUR SOUL

Come to me, all you who are weary and burdened, and I will give you rest. Take my yoke upon you and learn from me, for I am gentle and humble in heart, and you will find rest for your souls. For my yoke is easy and my burden is light.

MATTHEW 11:28-30

How are you really doing? Are you okay, fine, good, busy? These four-letter words slip from our mouths on autopilot like a car on cruise control. We utter them at checkout stands, in church pews, and in text messages to our friends next to smiling heart emojis. If we were honest, the words we'd sometimes like to use are *not okay*, *terrible*, *surviving*, and *exhausted*. These social pleasantries will never reveal the true state of your soul; there is always something deeper beneath its surface. Maybe you feel frazzled, strung out, burned out, and worn out. Maybe social media has made you feel like a stranger to your life. Maybe you feel like you are wasting the precious borrowed breaths God has given you.

We don't want to bother anyone with our true emotions or the soap opera of our lives, so we stay tight-lipped, put on a slight smile, and hide behind pretty and polished photos on our social media accounts.

Distraction, perfectionism, and addiction are how we cope. You might not feel like you can bring your burdens to anyone, but you can bring them to God. You might not feel like you can be your real self and share your real struggles and real emotions, but you can be real before God. He'll never block, mute, or unfollow you. You will never tire Him out with your true emotions—even those you think are ugly.

C. S. Lewis said, "The soul is but a hollow which God fills."[1] When you return to God, He promises to bring your soul back to life: "He makes me lie down in green pastures. He leads me beside still waters. He restores my soul" (Psalm 23:2-3, ESV). *The Message* interpretation of Jesus' words in Matthew 11:28 says, "Are you tired? Worn out? Burned out on religion? Come to me. Get away with me and you'll recover your life. I'll show you how to take a real rest. Walk with me and work with me—watch how I do it. Learn the unforced rhythms of grace. I won't lay anything heavy or ill-fitting on you. Keep company with me and you'll learn to live freely and lightly." God wants you to live freely and lightly in His presence, to keep company with Him, to walk in the rhythms of grace, and to receive a real rest.

But how can we keep company with God within the company of hundreds of thousands, millions of people we've never met in an artificial, virtual, pixelated world? We weren't made to watch strangers, acquaintances, celebrities, influencers, and even our friends' lives unfold in perfectly curated filtered photos and poorly produced fifteen-second video clips. We weren't made to listen to thousands of voices sharing their innermost feelings and documenting every moment of their day. We were made to be wide awake to our messy, ordinary, extraordinary lives.

So how is your soul, really? When we don't care for our souls, we fill the hollowness with endless scrolling, toxic relationships, too much food, drugs, alcohol, shopping, TV shows, movie marathons, and the addiction of our choice. But your soul wasn't made to be immersed in the vanities and shallow things of life; it was designed for depth and meaning.

The world can't offer us peace. To find rest for our souls, we must undress them of the ill fittings of this world: busyness, stress, envy, consumerism, chaos, strife, and toxic people and things. Instead, we must put on God's peace and saturate our souls with His living light. When we get weary again, we can run away from the clamoring noises of the world and sprint to His presence and find rest. We can rise again with the sun of a new day to find new mercies every morning. We can clothe ourselves with God's unceasing and steadfast love (see Lamentations 3:22-23, ESV) and walk in His grace-filled ways on the path to peace and fullness of joy. God has set eternity in our hearts, and heaven is where our souls will finally be restored (see Ecclesiastes 3:11), but even in this weary world, He is our refuge and can give us peace.

How is your soul, really?

God's love is wide and deep, vast and never-ceasing. He lavishes it upon you and calls you His child, friend, masterpiece, and the crowning creation of all He has made. He is "the fountain of life" (Psalm 36:9), a fountain we are thirsting for. He stands ready and waiting to restore your soul, which needs urgent and tender care. We need more of God and less of the world. We must put on stillness, silence, solitude, worthiness, and grace. Then, we'll move freely and lightly, like a day spent in our favorite buttery leggings.

Your Creator wants you to marvel at the miracle of your existence in wonder, to slow down and guzzle in every good and perfect gift He bestows on you. There is no such thing as an ordinary life. You have been lovingly and wonderfully created with awe, dignity, and immeasurable worth. You have been made to have a soul at rest.

You don't have to clean yourself up or tidy your soul to come to God. This is your invitation to unearth the life you've been made for, to live freely and lightly in His presence. It's an invitation only you can accept. This is your one shot at life. What do you want to do with it? What does your soul need this hour, this season, and what is it searching for?

Reflect

Circle all the words that describe the state of your soul:

Joyful, Peaceful, Content, Fulfilled, Harmonious, Compassionate, Enlightened, Grateful, Serene, Connected, Purposeful, Radiant, Liberated, Balanced, Loving, Blissful, Vibrant

Tattered, Weary, Desolate, Broken, Empty, Irritable, Wounded, Struggling, Sorrowful, Burdened, Lost, Fragmented, Drained, Melancholic, Anxious, Fearful

Use one adjective to describe your mental frame of mind when you wake up.

_____

Use one adjective to describe what frame of mind you want to be in when you wake up.

_____

What are the burdens of your life that you need to bring to God?

_____
_____

Pray

God, thank You for coming to rescue me from this world. Thank You for Your promise to restore my life and renew my soul. Help me run away from the chaos of this world; teach me to keep company with You, put on Your rhythms of grace, and live whole and free in Your loving presence.

Act

Do one small compassionate self-care practice today that will renew your spirit.

DAY 2

YOUR WILD AND PRECIOUS LIFE

The greatest surprise in my life is the brevity of life.
BILLY GRAHAM

David, the psalmist, asked God to impress upon him the brevity of his life: "Show me, Lord, my life's end and the number of my days; let me know how fleeting my life is. You have made my days a mere handbreadth; the span of my years is as nothing before you. Everyone is but a breath, even those who seem secure" (Psalm 39:4-5). He pleaded, "Teach us to number our days, that we may gain a heart of wisdom" (Psalm 90:12). We are like a golden California poppy dancing in the high desert wind, clothed in splendor but quickly fading. "What is your life? You are a mist that appears for a little while and then vanishes" (James 4:14).

To live a good life, to live a life of beauty and greatness and depth, we must know how fleeting it is. Wisdom requires that we grasp how swiftly passing and sacred our lives are. If we don't, we'll live like fools in the shallows of life, immersed in meaningless vanities and pursuits King Solomon calls "a chasing after the wind" (Ecclesiastes 1:14). You can run and hustle swiftly after the wind, but it cannot be caught. We can chase human approval, fame, material wealth, and beauty, but they will soon be gone even if we catch them for a moment.

Something that made me reconsider my relationship with social media was putting in perspective how much time I would spend on it throughout my life, which came out to over five years. Seconds on social media become minutes, become hours, become days, become weeks, become years. Doomscrolling on social media is like "traveling paths that go nowhere, wandering in a maze of detours and dead ends" (Proverbs 2:15, MSG). The girl who started mindlessly using social media at thirteen for five hours a day until she turned into a silver-haired eighty-year-old woman would have exhausted fourteen years of her life in a digital abyss, never to get them back. Ten years is enough time to sail the world several times, travel to faraway places, write a small library of books, backpack the world, survey the Seven Wonders, save hundreds of girls from sex trafficking, create artistic masterpieces, start nonprofits, raise a family, and live an extraordinary life that leaves a beautiful legacy. Imagine all you could do with ten years of your life.

Imagine how beautiful your life could be.

Women like Amelia Earhart, who set out to be the first woman to fly across the world; Esther, who saved the entire Jewish race from genocide; and Rosa Parks, who was known as the mother of the Civil Rights Movement, are some of the heroic and brilliant women who went before us. They show us what we are capable of. We have been made to do hard and holy things and live lives of greatness. Not only does social media addiction cause serious mental health issues, but it also robs us of our creativity and wastes our brain cells, time, talents, and intellect. It keeps us from living out our purpose. As we waste our lives a swipe at a time, the world misses out on our true selves and the incredible contributions we can offer.

As Mary Oliver asks in her poem "The Summer Day," "Tell me, what is it you plan to do / with your one wild and precious life?"[1] How would you live your life if no one was watching and you had nothing to show for it on social media? With no likes to look for or followers to gain, how would you exhaust your only tour around this planet? How would you spend the hidden moments of your life? How would you like to feel when you woke up, and what would your ideal day look like? Who are the people, and what are the things that bring you joy? What do you want your legacy to be? Imagine how beautiful your life could be if you filled it with as much beauty and goodness as it could contain and then happily missed out on everything else.

The apostle Paul, a follower of Jesus who once persecuted Christians before his dramatic conversion, cautions believers in his letter to the Ephesians: "Be very careful, then, how you live—not as unwise but as wise, making the most of every opportunity" (Ephesians 5:15-16). We are to live with eyes wide open. We are urged to live with wisdom and make the most of every borrowed breath we are given. As we sojourn through this world, we must be on guard and fight for joy and peace.

God always offers us something better than the world. We are given an invitation to a better life. A well-lived life is one that has been fought for, a life defended from the shallows and vanities of this world. Every breath you breathe is borrowed; a new one is never promised. Your life is wild, precious, and irreplaceable. God is inviting you to savor and steward every breath He gives you and to make the most of your life, only leaving goodness and beauty behind. This is your one and only precious, fleeting, beautiful, irreplaceable life. What will you do with it?

Reflect

What do you want your legacy to be? What do you want people to say about you at your celebration of life ceremony after you've passed away?

If you could spend ten years of your life doing anything other than being on social media, what would you do?

_____

_____

_____

Imagine a perfect day without your phone or any technology. What would you do? Where would you go?

_____

_____

_____

Pray

Lord, You did not have to create me but chose to because You love me. Help me to number my days and live with wisdom. Turn my eyes away from worthless things and help me live an extraordinary life that leaves others in awe of You.

Act

Take some time to look at photographs of yourself throughout your entire life. Marvel at and praise God for the miracle of your precious life.

DAY 3

WONDERFULLY MADE

I praise you because I am fearfully and wonderfully made;
your works are wonderful, I know that full well.

PSALM 139:14

Your body is uniquely composed of about 37.2 trillion cells, each with a specific task.[1] Your brain contains around eighty-five billion neurons and is the most complex structure known to creation.[2] Your heart beats around one hundred thousand times a day and pumps around two thousand gallons of blood.[3] Your eyes can perceive about ten million different colors.[4] Your skeleton is composed of 206 bones, stronger than steel and denser than concrete.[5] And no one else in the world or all of history will ever have the same fingerprints as you, a testament to the unique and intentional way God created you. You are the crown of creation, the finishing touch on all that has been made.

Our sense of self-worth hinges on the belief that we are either here by divine design or inexplicably without any reasonable cause. If we believe a loving Creator has intentionally created us, it affirms we have inherent value that can never be taken. However, our self-worth and purpose are up for dispute if we're not sure how or why we got here or if we're supposed to be here at all. If you've never thought much about spiritual matters such as these, I hope you will continue on this journey with an open heart. I pray you discover how loved and valued you are by the God who chose you before the foundations of the world (see Ephesians 1:4).

You are not an accident or the result of random cosmic collisions. You were loved into existence. You have been lovingly and phenomenally created by a God who has planned all of your days before one of them has come to be. God did not have to create you. It is an honor to have a heartbeat and breath in your lungs.

Psalm 139 is a prayer in which the psalmist, a man named David, articulates God's extravagant love for him. This prayer of praise is also for us and affirms the intimate way God knows us as His masterpieces. The psalm begins, "You have searched me, LORD, and you know me. You know when I sit and when I rise; you perceive my thoughts from afar. You discern my going out and my lying down; you are familiar with all my ways. Before a word is on my tongue you, LORD, know it completely" (verses 1-4). This Scripture captures the deep way God knows each of us, both relationally and experientially. God understands and knows you better than you will ever know yourself.

The Hebrew word for "known" is *yada*. In the context of Psalm 139, it means that Yahweh, or God, knows us relationally and experientially—he knows us in the depth of our being.[6] It is the deepest kind of knowing there is. No one knows an invention like its inventor. No one knows a masterpiece like its artist. No one will know you fully, deeply, like the Creator who formed and fashioned you in the secret place and offers you the opportunity through faith to have your name written in His Book of Life.

After several more profound verses, Psalm 139 continues: "For you created my inmost being; you knit me together in my mother's womb. I praise you because I am fearfully [reverently and lovingly] and wonderfully made; your works are wonderful, I know that full well" (verses 13-14).

God intricately and intentionally created you with awe, love, purpose, dignity, and worth. Your inherent value rests in the single truth that God chose to create you. In Psalm 139, David acknowledges the miracle of his existence. He praises God for his life and agrees that God made him beautifully and wonderfully. We are invited to do the same and to declare that God's creation is good, including us—we are the crowning glory of His creation; the finishing touch on all He has made.

Later, the psalmist is in awe that God's eyes saw his unformed body. All his days were written in God's book before one of them came to be (see Psalm 139:16). He reflects on the innumerable loving thoughts God has toward him that "outnumber the grains of sand" (Psalm 139:18). You can't run away from His presence; there isn't anywhere you can go that He won't be too. If you drift away, if you rise on the wings of the dawn, if you travel to the far side of the sea, He is there. If darkness seems to hide you, it will become like day because the dark can't overcome His light (see Psalm 139:7-12).

The world assaults our worth from every angle, and we must fight against the assaults every day. Today, social media is the arena where it seems we're losing this battle more than anywhere else. When we're lost in social media and trapped by comparison, we lose sight of our immeasurable and unshakable value. We fall asleep to the miracle of our one and only precious life. We spend our fleeting moments looking at the lives of friends and strangers, and as we do, we miss out on our own. The more we turn away from our Creator and look to other people, the more we worship and idolize them instead of the God who made us all equally and beautifully in His image.

We are here by divine design.

To live wide awake to the wonder of our life and in awe of the God who created us before the foundations of the world, we must keep returning to him daily. We cannot feel enveloped in this supernatural, boundless love if, day after day, moment after moment, we return to a pixelated, synthetic screen that endlessly loops the highlight reels of friends and strangers.

I hope that as you step away from social media, you will marvel at the miracle of your life. I hope you begin to believe in the depths of your heart that you are wonderfully made with a purpose no one else but you can fulfill. I hope you turn away from people and turn to the God who created and loves you more than you can ever fathom.

Reflect

Spend some time reflecting on the miracle of your life and the incredible way God made you.

What do you learn about God and His love for you through Psalm 139?

_____
_____
_____

How does social media make you focus on other people's lives and forget the miracle of your life?

_____
_____
_____

Pray

God, thank You for Your deep love for me. Thank You that You lovingly and wonderfully created me in Your image and gave me the gift of life. Help me turn away from other people and fix my gaze on You as the author and sustainer of my life.

Act

Write down some amazing things your body allows you to do, and thank God for your life.

_____
_____
_____

DAY 4

THE TRUEST THING ABOUT YOU

See what great love the Father has lavished on us, that we should be called children of God! And that is what we are!

1 JOHN 3:1

We can spend a lifetime searching for the answer to one of the deepest questions of our soul, *Who am I?* We look to people and things to answer this question—to give us validation, worth, and identity. We can turn to social media to determine what others think of us, our accomplishments, titles, appearance, or popularity. We can have a wardrobe of different identities we try on to find what gives us the most value in the eyes of the world. When we find our worth in false and fleeting identities, they can be taken from us at any moment, leaving us unsure of who we are without them. We need a solid, unshakable identity to build our lives on.

Brennan Manning said, "Define yourself radically as one beloved by God; God's love for you and his choice of you constitute your worth. Accept that, and let it become the most important thing in your life."[1] This is an identity that cannot be shaken. Your titles will come and go. Your talents and beauty will fade. Your relationships will change and end. Your self-esteem will go up and down when you compare yourself to others, focusing on comments, likes, and follows. But God's love for you and the identity He gives you through faith as His child will never change. This is who you are.

The truest, most definitive, most preeminent thing about you is that you are God's chosen and beloved child in whom He delights. God has loved you with an everlasting love (see Jeremiah 31:3). God did not have to create you, but He believed this world would not be complete without you. He chose you before the foundations of the world. He dreamed you up in His heart, knit you together in the secret place, and breathed you into existence. There never has been, and there will never be another you. You are God's original masterpiece, and He loves you more than you'll ever know.

God came down to us as fully God and fully man through His Son, the sinless person of Jesus Christ, bridging the gap between heaven and earth and revealing His true character and love for us. Jesus gave His life for you so that you could be forgiven, made new, set free, and have eternal life. How extravagantly loved you are!

This is the journey of becoming God's beloved— the journey of becoming who we really are.

The search to "find ourselves" will fail. We cannot find ourselves, but we have been found in God. We discover our true selves as we meet God personally in Jesus and let Him overtake our lives. As we become more like Christ and bear His image to the world, we become the fully alive and radiant women we've been made to be.

Your "belovedness" as a child of God is your birthright. There has never been a moment when you have not been loved by the Lord. No matter what you've done or how broken you are, you cannot escape and outrun God's love for you: "Nothing can ever separate us from God's love. Neither death nor life, neither angels nor demons, neither our fears for today nor our worries about tomorrow—not even the powers of hell can separate us from God's love. No power in the sky above or in the earth below—indeed, nothing in all creation will ever be able to separate us from the love of God that is revealed in Christ Jesus our Lord" (Romans 8:38-39, NLT).

There are four steps on our journey of becoming who we really are as God's beloved.

- First, we must discover God's love, which happens in many ways. It can come from someone's words or deeds; the reading of Scripture; the majesty of creation; a song, book, or movie; the whisper of God; a transformative spiritual experience; or the building of these throughout a lifetime. Through all these occurrences, God courts us with His love and patiently waits for us to respond.
- Next, we must believe. Through faith, like children, we receive the boundless gift of our Creator's love and surrender our lives to Him. Then, we abide in His love. We walk closely with Christ, hide our hearts in His, and dwell in His presence. We must defend ourselves from the assaults that tell us we are unworthy of this love.
- Then, we can embody our "belovedness," release our false identities, and live into our true, immovable identity as the beloved, letting it shape our every thought and action. Abiding in God's love will change how we show up in the world.
- Finally, we will effortlessly reveal the belovedness in others. We go and tell and show them that they have also been lavished by God's love and are invited through faith to become His children. This is the journey of becoming God's beloved—the journey of becoming who we really are.

Walking securely in our identity as God's children is a daily spiritual struggle. Henri Nouwen says, "The world tells you many lies about who you are, and you simply have to be realistic enough to remind yourself of this. . . . 'The truth, even though I cannot feel it right now, is that I am the chosen child of God, precious in God's eyes, called the Beloved from all eternity, and held safe in an everlasting embrace.'"[2]

The loudmouthed lies we hear from our spiritual enemy's whisper and the lips of others, and the ones running through our minds, try to strip us of our true identity. We can turn to a virtual world to find love and a sense of self-worth, but we will only find it in God. It takes faith to believe who we really are, which is being assaulted daily. God's love is so great and so vast that He calls us His children if we confess with our mouths and believe in our hearts that Jesus is Lord. No matter what we do, we will never stop being loved by God.

God also calls us His friends (see John 15:15). "Greater love has no one than this: to lay down one's life for one's friends" (John 15:13). Jesus has laid down His life for you and given you the gift of everlasting life and forgiveness if you choose to receive it. God does not want religion from you. He wants a relationship with you. Knowing and believing the profound depth of your worth and God's vast love for you can forever change your life and how you see yourself.

God is the author of your life and the source of your value. He is worthy of your heart. To be alive is to be loved by God. Live loved. Hold your head high. You are God's beloved, and that is the truest thing about you.

Reflect

What roles, people, or things do you find a sense of value and identity in?

How do you want other people to perceive or define you? Is this important to you? Why or why not?

Have you tried to perform for your worth or to please other people? If so, why do you think this is?

_____

_____

_____

Pray

Loving Father, thank You for giving me an unshakable identity as Your beloved child. Help me let go of the things I have placed my value in and cling tightly to my identity and worth as Your daughter. Reveal yourself to me in a greater way as I seek to live a life of lasting beauty, purpose, and significance.

Act

Take a few minutes to imagine your life if you lost important roles or relationships, experienced poor health, or no longer had things that give you a sense of self and value. Now, picture yourself being enveloped in God's love without these things.

DAY 5

COMING HOME

GOD's a safe-house for the battered, a sanctuary during bad times. The moment you arrive, you relax; you're never sorry you knocked.

PSALM 9:9-10, MSG

We all look for "home," searching for people, things, and places that will welcome us in the finest and foulest moments of our lives. We want to find a place we belong—somewhere people won't run away if they really knew us, somewhere we can stop hustling for our worth and exhale, somewhere that's a refuge from the storms that beat us down. Friend, stop right now. Take a deep breath. Let your thoughts linger here for a moment as I ask you some questions: What do you really want? What have you been searching for on social media but have not found? What does your soul need right now? What places have you been searching for "home" but not finding it? On social media, I sought to be seen, believing human approval would make me feel enough. But it never did.

I've heard that a parable is an earthly story with a heavenly meaning. Jesus told a lot of them. God's fatherly heart is revealed in the parable of the Prodigal Son. There was a rich man with two sons. The younger son came to his father and asked for his inheritance, then went to faraway lands and indulged in wild and lavish living until he squandered everything. A famine came, leaving him in poverty. With nowhere else to go, he staggered home, hoping he could at least be one of his father's servants. But the father was overtaken with joy and ran to embrace his son. He said, "Let's have a feast and celebrate. For this son of mine was dead and is alive again; he was lost and is found" (Luke 15:23-24).

> When we come home to God and come home to our lives, we find soul-deep rest.

I'm sure the son lived it up when he first left home. It's fun to do whatever we want and live how we please—until we face the consequences of doing life apart from God. The ways of the world are like a wild, raging music festival in the Southern California desert. It's fun for a while until you get trampled or thrown up on. If we're honest with ourselves, we're really searching for love, peace, and belonging, and the world only offers knockoff versions of these desires.

Nonstop highlight reels can make it look like others are living it up and enjoying life more than you are, but we never have the full story. They can make us feel like our lives are ordinary when they are extraordinary. But when we come home to God and come home to our lives, we find soul-deep rest no number of likes or follows will ever provide.

Taking the crowded, wide road to pleasure and self-indulgence is exhilarating and enticing, but it is a dead end. Heartbreak and destruction await. But the ways of God that bring us home restore our souls as the psalmist declares: "You make known to me the path of life; in your presence there is fullness of joy; at your right hand are pleasures forevermore" (Psalm 16:11, ESV). Goodness and love follow us all the days of our lives as we find our home in God (see Psalm 23:6).

What have you done that you are ashamed of? Do you believe God won't love you because of the things you've done? Are you worried He won't welcome you for the first time or take you back? You are never too far gone. I'm sorry if your earthly father abandoned you or let you down. But God is different. He is our perfect Father. He is always faithful, slow to anger, and abounding in unconditional love and compassion. His heart breaks when His children wander and run away. But He rejoices when they come back home. The world won't love you broken, but Jesus will run to you. You'll never find what you're really looking for on your phone, but you'll find more than you could have imagined in the loving embrace of the God who made you.

In this parable, Jesus reveals His heart—the heart of God, the heart of the One who loves you at your finest and foulest moments, the heart of the One who will always welcome you home, the heart of the One who has chosen you before the foundations of the world. Jesus is our refuge in this weary world, but our true citizenship is in heaven (see Philippians 3:20). He promised us that He has gone to prepare a home for us in heaven where there are many rooms for us (see John 14:2). Through faith in Christ, we can dwell in His house forever and belong to the family of God (see Psalm 23:6).

Nothing can separate you from the love of Jesus (see Romans 8:38-39). He has taken on shame so that you don't have to. He will always welcome you back. And when you return, He will run to you and throw a party because you were lost and now are found. You were dead, but now you are alive. We can wander, but God won't wander from us. No matter what you've done or how far from God you feel, He is waiting for you to return. He is all you have been searching for, and He can't wait to welcome you home.

Reflect

What does "home" represent to you?

_____

_____

_____

_____

What are you searching for, and what have you been looking for on social media?

_____

_____

_____

What are the wrong places and who are the wrong people you've been running to in your search for love and belonging?

_____

_____

_____

Pray

God, thank You that nothing I do can separate me from Your love. Thank You for running to me even in my worst moments and for always welcoming me home. Help me to turn away from the wide and destructive road of the world and find refuge in Your love.

Act

Make a list of three activities that help you feel close to God. Pick one to do today.

_____

_____

_____

DAY 6

BE THE DECORATOR OF YOUR LIFE

Turn my eyes from looking at worthless things; and give me life in your ways.

PSALM 119:37, ESV

God is the architect and overseer of our lives. He designed and envisioned us before we came to be: "Before [He] formed you in the womb [He] knew you" (Jeremiah 1:5). His Word and precepts are like the blueprints of our lives, giving us guidance and a solid foundation to build on. But we are the interior decorators of our lives. We have the freedom to decide how to adorn them.

We alone get to decide what we will fill our lives with—who we will entrust our hearts to, what we will look at and listen to, what we will surround ourselves with, how we will spend our time, and what we will pursue with the days we've been given. If we want to flourish and live our best life possible, we must invite the light of Christ to shine upon us so we can become master designers of our lives and fill them with as much beauty as they can contain. Will we let darkness or light into the home of our souls? Will we let them be filthy or clean? God is our builder, our creator, but we design the interior of our lives.

We get to decide what will guide us. Evil and darkness are all around us, but so are good and light, beauty and wonder. Jesus gave us wisdom for a thriving and wholehearted life: "The eye is the lamp of the body. If your eyes are healthy, your whole body will be full of light. But if your eyes are unhealthy, your whole body will be full of darkness" (Matthew 6:22-23).

Our eyes are like windows that fill our souls with light or darkness. If we gaze upon the good, lovely, true, and beautiful things of life, we will be radiant. Our lives will overflow with goodness—our minds will be clear, our words will be pleasant, and our souls will be content. But if we look at the darkness and evil of our world, our lives will be void of light. They will lack joy and peace.

What we gaze at with our little eyes and what we listen to with our little ears will determine the state of our souls. The movies we watch, the TV shows we binge, the lyrics we sing, and the people we do life with will influence who we are. All we take in will shape our character and who we become.

Proverbs 4:23 tells us, "Above all else, guard your heart, for everything you do flows from it." From our hearts come our thoughts, beliefs, and actions. We must become gatekeepers standing watch against the attacks of our spiritual enemy. We must protect ourselves from the onslaughts of the world.

Fill your life with as much goodness and beauty as it can contain.

Social media and the internet can be a keyhole to deplorable people and images. With the tap of your finger, you can see the worst of the world. We cannot unsee the things we see and unhear the things we hear—every second online matters. Every sight and every sound leaves a mark on us. What we allow into our lives will eventually come out. Our inputs become our outputs.

We were not designed to bear the burdens of the entire world. As if the stresses, demands, and struggles of our own lives are not unbearable enough, we crumble under the weight of all the problems of the world and the noise of other people's lives. Social media algorithms elevate content that will give us a visceral response, sucking us in as we doomscroll through life. For some people, exposure to the news and social media has a tremendously negative effect on well-being and results in heightened levels of depression, hopelessness, and anxiety.[1]

By eliminating our exposure to damaging inputs of sights, sounds, and voices, we give ourselves space to enjoy the better things in life. We take responsibility for our mental and spiritual well-being when we diligently guard our hearts. When we focus on our circle of control, decide to seek all that is good, and turn away from what is bad, we can live fully alive and burst with light in body and soul.

God always invites us into a better life. His precepts or desires for how we should live are "right, giving joy to the heart" (Psalm 19:8). They revive our souls. The ways of God we are invited to follow are good and pure: "The path of the righteous is like the morning sun, shining ever brighter till the full light of day" (Proverbs 4:18). The ways of the world we are tempted to travel on are dark and evil: "The way of the wicked is like deep darkness; they do not know what makes them stumble" (Proverbs 4:19). We find soul-deep rest and joy in the ways of God, but death and destruction await us in the ways of the world. Only we can decide what path to take.

Imagine what your life could be like if you spent your days gazing upon the beauty of God and all He has made. Fill your life with as much goodness and beauty as it can contain. Enjoy the loveliest things of life—the happiest people, the best scents, the most stunning sights, the most delightful music, the comfiest clothes. Light your favorite scented candle, pick fresh flowers, play music that soothes your soul, talk to your best friend, and cozy up with your favorite blanket while drinking your favorite coffee in your favorite mug. Chase beauty every day and catch it. Bottle up all the good gifts this life bestows. Inhale truth, light, beauty, and joy. Exhale your concerns.

Guard your heart and mind and protect your innermost being. We can look at God or the world, light or darkness, good or evil. As we turn our eyes away from worthless things, we can set our hearts upon all that is good and everlasting. Ask God to help you become a master designer of your life and watch it overflow with beauty, joy, and peace.

Reflect

List the negative voices and things in your life.

_____

_____

_____

List the loveliest people and things that bring you joy and peace.

_____

_____

_____

What can you turn away from, and what can you turn toward that will allow you to design a more beautiful and peaceful life?

_____

_____

Pray

God, help me take responsibility for guarding my heart. Help me fill my life with truth and goodness. Empower me to turn away from darkness, and give me life as I walk in Your ways, which lead to peace and the fullness of joy.

Act

Make a list of three things you want to infuse into your life or create an inspiring vision board with images and words that evoke the goodness and beauty you want more of in your life.

_____

_____

_____

DAY 7

PULLING WEEDS

The LORD will guide you always; he will satisfy your needs in a sun-scorched land and will strengthen your frame. You will be like a well-watered garden, like a spring whose waters never fail.

ISAIAH 58:11

If your life were a garden, what would it be teeming with? What is blooming, and what weeds are choking the life out of it? We are made to tend to the garden of our lives and pull the weeds that keep us from living abundantly. As we do, we blossom and become fully alive.

In order to transform our lives, we must identify these "weeds"—the habits, addictions, false beliefs, actions, and people that keep us from thriving. Ask yourself, "What isn't working for me? What is sucking the life out of me? What is keeping me from the life I dream of?" Common weeds in our lives can include stress, addictions, unhealthy relationships, shame, bad habits, strongholds, limiting beliefs, and self-destructive patterns. I hope this reset is giving you the space to identify the weeds in your life and consider if social media is one that is keeping you from fully blooming.

In addition to these common weeds, sin robs us of a flourishing life. We all mess up. *Sin* is a religious word we can dislike or dismiss. But to sin means we miss the mark, do things that dishonor God, and go against His loving precepts and desires for the way He wants us to live. Every one of us falls short of the goodness and glory of God. We all sin, and every sinner is equal in God's sight. It's not pleasant to admit we are sinners, but we all are, and there is no shame in this; it makes God's grace and forgiveness even more necessary and beautiful.

Among other things, Scripture calls out the sins of "sexual immorality, impurity and debauchery; idolatry and witchcraft; hatred, discord, jealousy, fits of rage, selfish ambition, dissensions, factions and envy; drunkenness, orgies, and the like" (Galatians 5:19-21). God wants the best for us, and these sins keep us from flourishing because of the destruction they bring. They steal life from our souls and keep us from the blessings of God.

Trust God as the master gardener of your life.

When scattered throughout the garden of our lives like invasive weeds, these things keep us from thriving and lead to death and destruction. But we are made for a flourishing life. When we abide in God, His Spirit overtakes the parts of us that dishonor and displease Him. We begin to blossom with the fruit of the Spirit: "love, joy, peace, forbearance [patience], kindness, goodness, faithfulness, gentleness and self-control" (Galatians 5:22-23). These character traits come from abiding in God and practicing His ways, which lead to life and joy.

During Bible times, people worked and lived off the land. The Scriptures talk a lot about sowing and reaping. To sow means to put seeds in the ground. To reap is to cut and collect a grain crop. Spiritually speaking, we will reap what we sow in our lives (see Galatians 6:7), which offers hope that we can improve our lives. If we sow peace, we will reap joy. If we sow obedience, we will reap blessings. And if we sow faith, we will reap hope. Ask God to empower you to sow beauty and goodness in your life. Wait patiently, and a harvest of abundance will envelop you.

Continually sowing what is good and rooting out everything that doesn't bring life is the secret to a wholehearted life. But just like pulling weeds once doesn't get rid of them forever, we must continually examine our lives and rid them of everything that keeps us from thriving. The more you weed a garden, the more it blooms. The more we pull the weeds in our lives, the more we blossom and the more beautiful our lives become.

We can't get free on our own from what keeps us from flourishing. We must be rooted in God as our source of life. We must rely on His grace and supernatural strength that is made perfect in our weakness. Each weed you pull leaves space to sow something that will reap something better. Getting free from an addiction will bring life and peace. Ending a toxic relationship will restore your dignity. Healing from an eating disorder will save your life. Stopping the habit of numbing through the escape of your choice, such as overusing social media, will give you your life back.

Imagine what your life could look like if you pulled your most destructive weeds and planted something beautiful in their place. How would you be different? Identify these weeds and ask for the supernatural strength to pull them. This is hard and holy work. It can look like going to rehab or counseling, joining a support group, ending a relationship, or breaking a bad habit. Social media can be an unnecessary stressor and a weed we're better off without. By the end of your reset, you may decide you even need to extend your time away from social media or get off of it completely. Changing our lives requires sacrifices, but friend, you can do hard things because great is the power of God in you.

The journey toward an abundant, overflowing life is about ridding your life of all the junk and replacing it with as much beauty and goodness as you can. Trust God as the master gardener of your life. When you abide in Him as a branch abides in a vine, you will bear fruit. As you remain in Christ and make your home in Him, you will flourish, bloom, and have a life more beautiful than you could ever imagine.

Reflect

Pause, close your eyes, and envision the garden of your life. Write down the answer to these questions:

What is blooming?

_____

_____

What are the weeds that are choking the life out of you?

_____

_____

_____

What would you like to plant in the garden of your life that will help you bloom where you are planted?

_____

_____

_____

Pray

God, thank You for coming to give me a flourishing life. Help me identify the things choking life, peace, and joy from me. Help me turn away from sin, abide in You, and cultivate the fruit of the Spirit in my life.

Act

Make a commitment and a plan to eliminate one "weed" from your life today.

DAY 8

THE BEAUTY OF AN UNSEEN LIFE

Be careful not to practice your righteousness in front of others to be seen by them. If you do, you will have no reward from your Father in heaven.

MATTHEW 6:1

There are no secrets on social media. I try really hard not to look at the Search & Explore section of Instagram. It's a dangerous place for me to wander, so it's better if I keep my distance. But every time I fall into its trap, it slaps me with reminders of the things I don't have.

Spellbound, one day, within a vulnerable minute of scrolling through the lives of strangers, I saw a woman taking a pregnancy test and screaming for joy when it tested positive, a girl doing her workout routine in matching buttery-soft leggings and a sports bra while I was eating leftover pizza, a woman getting dressed in a walk-in closet bigger than my first apartment, a couple embracing in their kitchen, and a girl reading her Bible while it was still dark outside. It seems like everyone is living out loud, and if you don't live in a way that captivates the world's attention, it isn't good enough.

But as He always does, God invites us into a better, though unpopular, way of life. We are advised, "Make it your ambition to lead a quiet life: You should mind your own business" (1 Thessalonians 4:11). Our culture's collective ambition is to live loudly—to generate as much attention and accumulate as much wealth and fame as possible. It teaches us that we need more followers, a blue verified check next to our name, and a bigger platform to be successful.

This brings the temptation to live for human approval at the expense of our souls. Jesus warns us: "What good will it be for someone to gain the whole world, yet forfeit their soul? Or what can anyone give in exchange for their soul?" (Matthew 16:26). Living for likes and follows and for human approval can bring all the power, fame, wealth, and pleasure the world has to offer, but it can come at the expense of peace and joy.

In the Gospels, we see the great lengths Jesus went to in order to avoid crowds. He was faithful to love, heal, and save people, but he ran away from fame and sought refuge in solitude with God, His Father.

> *What would you choose if you had to pick between being seen by the world or being known by God?*

Whether or not we have a big platform or personality, we are invited to a deep, spiritually quiet, and faithful life. God's love, not the attention of others, will give us the fullness of joy we crave, the soul-deep rest that comes simply from being a child of God.

There is beauty and power in a private life—a life that is secret and unseen by the rest of the world but known and seen by God and the people you love the most. There are holy and sacred moments only you, God, and the people you love most should see. Who are you in the unseen moments of your life? How would you live if you could have the best life you can imagine but have nothing to show for it on social media?

Living a quiet life does not mean that you can't have an outgoing personality, be an extrovert, make an impact, have a big platform, or achieve your dreams. Even if you are a social media influencer doing big things that are seen by the world, living a "quiet" life is about being faithful in the big and small unseen moments of our lives. It's about having integrity. It's about your character and who you are when the world isn't watching.

This way of life allows us to dig deep and put down hidden roots that will help us flourish and withstand the storms of life: "That person is like a tree planted by streams of water, which yields its fruit in season and whose leaf does not wither—whatever they do prospers" (Psalm 1:3). But the lives of those not rooted and established in God "are like chaff that the wind blows away" (Psalm 1:4). When we make it our life's mission to please God by living a faithful life and believe in the depths of our souls that we are seen and known and loved by Him, we are firmly established and cannot be moved.

The world teaches us to hide our sins and brokenness and parade our good deeds. God teaches the opposite—to confess our sins to one another so that we may be healed and to hide our righteousness so that people won't see it, but only God in secret. An unseen life allows God and others to be our publicists, deciding when our successes, deeds, and qualities will be illuminated. While an unseen and quiet life won't generate as much fame or as many followers, it will give your soul peace.

When we fall for the trappings of this world and live for human approval, we experience strife and emptiness. God wants to give us rest for our souls away from the crowds in His life-giving presence. What would you choose if you had to pick between being seen by the world or being known by God? Do you want fame or a soul at rest? Do you want to chase human approval or find joy in God's unconditional love? What kind of life do you want to live?

Reflect
What kind of life does the world pressure you to live?

What kind of person do you want to be when no one is watching?

What would it look like to stop living for human approval and live in a way that honors God, even if it doesn't get much attention on social media or from other people?

Pray

God, help me to live a faithful life with everything You've given me. Empower me to become the woman You want me to be when no one is watching. Thank You for loving and knowing and seeing me. Thank You that my value comes from You alone.

Act

Do one act of kindness for someone in secret that honors God and blesses someone.

DAY 9

THE STRENGTH OF SOLITUDE AND SILENCE

In quietness and trust is your strength.
ISAIAH 30:15

In a noisy and distracting world, God politely whispers, inviting us to find refuge from the chaos of our lives through the practice of solitude and silence. He does not shout to make Himself heard above the unnecessary chatter. He is that "still, small voice" eager to give you rest from a world constantly vying for your attention. Jesus modeled solitude for us, as we see in the Gospels. He regularly withdrew from the crowd to spend time alone with God.

Solitude and silence are spiritual disciplines that revive our weary souls. They require hard work and sacrifice, but their reward is great. Solitude is the state of intentionally being alone or isolated with the goal of drawing closer to God. It gives us time and space for reflection, introspection, and spiritual growth. It is different from loneliness. Loneliness is the feeling of being disconnected from others, which negatively affects our mental health, but solitude is an intentional spiritual practice that restores us.

While we don't need to run away from our day-to-day lives to experience solitude, Dallas Willard writes, "In solitude, we purposefully abstain from interaction with other human beings, denying ourselves companionship and all that comes from our conscious interaction with others. We close ourselves away; we go to the ocean, to the desert, the wilderness, or to the anonymity of the urban crowd. . . . Solitude is choosing to be *alone* and to dwell on our experience of isolation from other human beings. Solitude frees us."[1]

The practice of solitude reduces stress and anxiety, enhances creativity, and improves decision-making in relationships.[2] I've personally found that it makes me more emotionally resilient and mentally healthy. Solitude forces us to sit silently with our own souls. For some, it is a painful thing to be avoided at all costs through distraction and addiction, and endless scrolling can be our escape of choice. Solitude allows us to enter into the loving presence of our Creator, who is the sustainer of our lives. There is no substitute that can restore our souls the way abiding in the love of Christ will.

In a noisy and distracting world, God politely whispers.

When we get quiet and alone and close ourselves off from the world, we are forced to face the emptiness in our souls we've been filling with noise, busyness, people, and the numbing habit of our choice. This experience can be quite unpleasant and even painful, leading us to look for an instant escape, but this tension makes the practice of solitude even more necessary. Social media is an ever-present escape drug, making the gift of solitude one that can go unopened; a gift that is sure to restore our souls.

Solitude is not a one-time experience but a practice that must be returned to again and again. In the presence of the Holy Spirit, our Wonderful Counselor, we are freed from our pain, emotional wounds, and anxieties. Second Corinthians 3:17 says, "Now the Lord is the Spirit, and where the Spirit of the Lord is, there is freedom." Solitude allows us to be still and know that God is God (see Psalm 46:10).

If we want to be well, we must run away from the chaos of social media. We must deliberately shut the door to the noise of the world and the clamoring voices surrounding us. Solitude requires silence. In silence, we lock our souls inside from the noise of the outside world—from wars and rumors of wars, from comparison, from the trappings of the world, and from the opinions of others.

Silence requires that we take action to delete the app, turn off the television and our notifications, and hush the crushing sounds and the voices of others. There will be great resistance, but the reward is great. Dallas Willard writes, "Silence is frightening because it strips us as nothing else does, throwing us upon the stark realities of our life."[3] If we must always be enveloped by noise, it indicates that there may be an inward emptiness we soothe with distraction, loud voices, and sounds. If you find solitude and silence to be painful, your soul might be trying to tell you something.

If we conform to the chaos of the world and play along with the social media circus, we will never know God's good, perfect, and pleasing will for our lives. Only through the spiritual disciplines of solitude and silence will we hear God's whisper and find soul-deep rest.

I hope this reset is ushering you into peace. As you continue your social media reset, how can you use the extra hours in your day to practice solitude? What do you need to do to allow God to restore your soul and help you recover your life?

Reflect

What can you do to spend more time practicing the spiritual disciplines of solitude and silence?

What noise and distractions can you eliminate from your life?

THE STRENGTH OF SOLITUDE AND SILENCE

Where would you go if you could retreat somewhere to practice an extended time of solitude and silence?

Pray

God, I want to hear Your voice. Help me make choices to eliminate the noise and chaos around me. Help me set aside intentional time to draw close to You through solitude and silence. Restore my soul and set me free as I turn away from the noise and chaos of the world.

Act

Plan several minutes of solitude. Try to go somewhere away from the stress of your daily life and commitments.

DAY 10

A HEART AT REST

The LORD is my shepherd, I lack nothing.
PSALM 23:1

Tell me if this scenario sounds familiar: you're lying on the couch, zoning out with your phone out, scrolling through the latest posts on your feed, when an ad pops up with the exact shimmery foundation, pair of boots, or swimsuit you've been searching for. Like your personal shopper, the social media algorithms picked out a shiny new purchase just for you. They know exactly what you like. They know exactly what you want.

In a vulnerable moment of boredom, anxiety, or sadness, the purchase becomes irresistible, so you click "add to cart" and "buy," and it's on your doorstep forty-eight hours later. Shopping lights up the reward systems in our brains, gives us a fleeting dopamine hit, and provides momentary relief from stress and emotional uneasiness. Like many of us, I have fallen for one too many social media ads, leaving me with buyer's remorse over a worthless purchase. Like the time I bought a black, stretchy jumpsuit modeled by a cute, twirling influencer, which I could barely fit my right calf through.

Social media generates over $200 billion annually and counting from advertising, exploiting our sense of inadequacy and capitalizing on our ravenous desire for more stuff.[1] Social media companies collect vast amounts of data from users. This data includes demographic information, interests, pages liked, past posts you've interacted with, and websites you've visited. They use machine-learning algorithms to analyze your behavior and track the content you've engaged with to make predictions about your preferences.

This information is used to tailor targeted advertisements, which you are more likely to respond to. When the algorithms realize that you interact with certain kinds of ads, they will show you even more of them. Advertisements fool us into believing the product will make us better—that it will soothe our low self-worth. It's not so much the product we are buying but the false hope it promises and the positive feelings it evokes, which is often accomplished through beautiful influencers and good photography and branding. The more we're online, the more ads we see. The more ads we see, the more we want. The more we want, the more we buy, and the cycle of consumerism continues.

> Contentment is a posture of the heart.

The financial guru Dave Ramsey calls us out: "We buy things we don't need with money we don't have to impress people we don't like."[2] The high we get from buying new things is fleeting and never satisfies. Jesus said, "No one can serve two masters. Either you will hate the one and love the other, or you will be devoted to the one and despise the other. You cannot serve both God and money" (Matthew 6:24).

The constant desire for more can indicate an emotional or spiritual void in our lives. Just like other addictions and unhealthy coping mechanisms, the appetite for more possessions, status, and wealth can be an attempt to fill the God-shaped hole in our hearts.

Contentment is a state of peace and satisfaction. When you have a contented heart, your soul is at rest, and you live in a state of gratitude for everything you have. When you abide in God, you can be like Jesus' follower Paul, who said, "I know what it is to be in need, and I know what it is to have plenty. I have learned the secret of being content in any and every situation, whether well fed or hungry, whether living in plenty or in want" (Philippians 4:12). Contentment is something that must be learned and practiced.

The secret to contentment is something many people in our Western culture ensnared by consumerism never find. It is a state of gratitude for all we already have that quenches our thirst for more. Contentment is a posture of the heart that is not dependent on material possessions, status, wealth, or life circumstances. It's the belief that God has not withheld all we need.

Contentment is always better than having material wealth and possessions. Proverbs, the book of wisdom, tells us, "Better a little with the fear [love and respect] of the LORD than great wealth with turmoil" (15:16). Fame and material things do not lead to happiness and often come with a lot of problems—just look at the latest issue of *People* magazine.

Jesus told us, "Watch out! Be on your guard against all kinds of greed; life does not consist in an abundance of possessions" (Luke 12:15). Hebrews 13:5 says, "Keep your lives free from the love of money and be content with what you have, because God has said, 'Never will I leave you; never will I forsake you.'" Contentment requires that we trust God to provide for all our needs. It comes from dwelling in His presence and being grateful for every good and perfect gift we have. In God, we lack nothing (see Psalm 23:1). This posture of the heart says, "God, thank You. I love You, and You have given me everything I need. I trust You to provide and care for me."

In addition to gratitude, contentment also comes from the practice of self-denial. When we deny ourselves the opportunity to have everything we want as soon as we want it, we force ourselves to enjoy what we already have. Setting and following a budget, being generous, refusing to buy things on credit, spending less time buying items online, and taking periodic shopping fasts can quell our desire for more and cultivate a spirit of contentment that will be more satisfying than any shiny new purchase.

Jesus tells us, "Do not lay up for yourselves treasures on earth, where moth and rust destroy and where thieves break in and steal, but lay up for yourselves treasures in heaven, where neither moth nor rust destroys and where thieves do not break in and steal. For where your treasure is, there your heart will be also" (Matthew 6:19-21, ESV). Our culture delights in riches, fame, possessions, and temporary things that will pass away. Social media showcases and rewards those who have achieved these things. But they will rust and rot away.

When we practice contentment, earthly pleasures lose their appeal as we delight ourselves in the better things of God. We cannot take anything with us when we leave this world. Naked we come, naked we go. Only our legacy will be left behind. Don't fall for the disappointing trap of materialism and consumerism. How would you be different if you stopped filling the God-shaped hole in your heart with material things and instead practiced contentment? As you do, you will cultivate a heart at rest that brings life and peace to your soul.

Reflect

How have social media ads targeted you and increased your desire for more things?

Why do you think we live in such a culture of consumerism?

How has this culture and the pressure to be and have more impacted you?

Pray

God, thank You for giving me everything I need. Cultivate a contented heart within me. Help me to turn away from earthly pursuits and possessions and store treasures in heaven. Teach me to seek Your Kingdom first, and turn my eyes from worthless things.

Act

Take a break from shopping and spending money on things you don't need for the day or the rest of the week. Consider donating the money you save to a charity you care about.

DAY 11

LOOKING FOR LIKES, LONGING FOR LOVE

They loved human praise more than praise from God.
JOHN 12:43

A desire to be known is etched into the human soul. We cannot quell it, and we can be mistaken in believing that being seen and being known are the same thing. Social media provides us with the irresistible opportunity to be seen by anyone in the world. There's nothing like the dopamine hit we get from another like, comment, or follow. It's a quick, fleeting high that keeps us coming back for more.

It is fun to talk to friends, meet new people, show highlights from your day, and post happy moments of your life. It is amazing to be able to talk to anyone in the world and see updates from your friends. But living on your phone and posting to win human approval will leave you empty. Oversharing on social media can lead to negative self-esteem, stress, anxiety, negative body image, and hurtful comments, and it can threaten your privacy and safety. I can't count the number of times I've felt self-conscious and anxious after I've posted something on social media. More than once, I've gotten lost in my head, thinking about imaginary thoughts and judgments people might have about me and what I shared. Can you relate?

Constantly posting photos and videos of ourselves can cause us to think about ourselves too much, making us feel anxious, self-conscious, and exposed to the judgments of others. This is a common experience for women who use social media. Research has found that excessive selfie-taking leads to heightened self-objectification, negative mood, and lower self-esteem, which harms mental health.[1] Our desire to be seen and capture the perfect selfie or photo to post can distract us from the beauty of the present moment. When we are consumed by how we look in photos, we can become too self-focused, and it can distract us from making authentic, unposed memories.

If we're always looking to be seen, sometimes it means we have not had the deepest question of our souls—"Am I loved as I am and without condition?"—answered. To be seen and liked is to hold fool's gold. But to be known and loved is to have eternal riches.

> God loves, sees, and knows you. Return to Him and find a love you'll never outrun.

When we don't find our worth in God, we can do compromising things to get the attention we mistake for love. In the social media circus, we can look for likes while we long for love. It's like we're posting and asking the judges' panel, "Do you love me? Do you see me? Do you hear me? What do you think of me? Am I lovely? Am I beautiful?" We give others the power to tell us what we're worth. Proverbs 29:25 says, "Fear of man will prove to be a snare," which means when we're concerned with the opinions of others and are fixed on winning their approval, we can't be free.

We can be addicted to human approval so much that we search for likes from people we don't like! Acquaintances and strangers on the internet will never truly know us and won't always accept us. When we live to please others, we bend to their preferences and who they want us to be. We reject our true selves.

Imagine how different our lives could be if, instead of trying to impress other people, we were impressed by the goodness of God. With no applause to perform for, followers to attain, or likes to gain, how would you live your life?

We can't experience true love and peace in the company of a crowd of thousands of strangers on a screen. Peace requires turning away from the masses. We must run away from the clamoring noise of the world to quiet places where we can hear God's whisper, which will tell us that we are loved. He will gently remind you that you don't need to perform for your worth. He will tell you that you are cherished the same in the best and worst moments of your life. It's only in quietness, stillness, and solitude through a friendship with God that the cravings of your heart can be satisfied.

Even if you are unknown to the world and unknown on social media, you will never be unknown to God. You can either spend your life striving to be seen or believe you are not only seen but known and loved by God and make it your mission to see, know, and love others.

The love of the world will always come with conditions. God sees us—the good, the bad, and the ugly—and loves us anyway. A love that says, "I delight in you. Not for what you do, or how you look, or what you have, but for who you are." The love of God won't give you a dopamine hit the way a new like, comment, or follow will. But it will give you peace. It will give you a heart at rest. It will be the nourishment your soul is thirsting for. God loves, sees, and knows you. Return to Him and find a love you'll never outrun. This is the love no amount of likes or follows will ever compare to. This is the love you've been searching for.

Reflect

How do you relate to the desire to be seen on social media?

_____

_____

_____

_____

How is being seen and known by God different from being seen and known by others?

___

What can you do to remember that God knows you and that you don't have to perform for others' approval?

___

Pray

Thank You, God, that You see and know me. Teach me to find my value and identity in You and not live for human approval. Help me trust in Your love for me and not concern myself with what others may think of me.

Act

When and if you post on social media (after your reset), ask yourself your motives before you share something.

DAY 12

LADY WISDOM AND LADY FOLLY

Know also that wisdom is like honey for you: If you find it, there is a future hope for you, and your hope will not be cut off.

PROVERBS 24:14

In the book of Proverbs, we meet two allegorical women: Lady Wisdom and Lady Folly. Lady Wisdom is our role model, teaching us to sit at her feet and learn from her ways, but Lady Folly is her personified antagonist, luring us to do whatever we want and live to our heart's content. The Bible offers endless instructions on how to live wisely and warns us of the destruction that comes with foolishness. Proverbs can teach us how to live wisely on and off social media.

Written mostly by King Solomon, who is claimed to be the wisest man (after Jesus, of course), the book of Proverbs is a guidebook containing nine hundred short, poetic reflections on life, relationships, work, and how to live in the world. Proverbs is a guide for wise and wonderful living, which only comes from a love for God: "The fear [love and respect] of the Lord is the beginning of wisdom, and knowledge of the Holy One is understanding" (Proverbs 9:10).

Proverbs teaches us that wisdom is more worthy than wealth, success, beauty, or fame: "Wisdom is far more valuable than rubies. Nothing you desire can compare with it" (Proverbs 8:11, NLT). Proverbs 8:35 says, "For whoever finds me [wisdom] finds life, and obtains favor from the LORD" (NKJV). If we lack wisdom, we can ask God, who promises to give it to us generously (see James 1:5), but we must have receptive ears and an obedient heart.

Proverbs gives us insight into the curse of foolishness and the blessing of wisdom, and it is personified in chapters 7 and 8 through Lady Wisdom and Lady Folly.

These chapters tell us what Lady Folly is like: She does whatever she wants. Lady Folly is loud, seductive, and knows nothing (see Proverbs 9:13). She does not know how to tame her tongue, which gets her in a lot of trouble. She flaunts her body and beauty and follows her sexual desires without restraint. Like many of the women on and off social media and television, Lady Folly gets a lot of attention. Our world and social media can elevate Lady Folly, rewarding her with attention from men, likes, follows, verified blue checks, money, and fame. However, her lack of wisdom and discernment can lead her to make bad choices and even self-destruct.

We have two paths we can take: the path of foolishness or the path of wisdom.

Lady Wisdom, on the other hand, though she might not get as much attention, is to be honored. She has trustworthy things to say and speaks what is right; her mouth speaks what is true, and her lips detest wickedness; the words of her mouth are just, and none of them are perverse (see Proverbs 8:6-9). She has sound judgment, understanding, and power (see Proverbs 8:14). She walks in the way of truth, seeks justice, and has riches, honor, and prosperity. Her character and unfading beauty attract the attention of good and worthy men.

Lady Wisdom is further described through the "Wife of Noble Character" portrayed in Proverbs 31. This does not describe an actual woman but paints an ideal picture of feminine wisdom, giving us an example of virtue to aspire to: "This wise woman is rare and hard to find. Her value comes from her character, from the depths of who she is. This noble, virtuous woman values family, hard work, is a good steward of her resources, and is financially savvy, serving the needy and glorifying God with her life."[1]

In our culture, we are conditioned to believe we must live out loud, do things to get attention, and live to our heart's desire. But living counterculturally with wisdom on and off social media gives us a better life rich in peace and joy. If you choose to continue using it after your reset, ask yourself how you can use social media with wisdom in a God-honoring way that also respects yourself. How can you show up in a way that doesn't cause shame or regret and reflects the kind of woman you want to be that is aligned with your God-given worth?

The allegorical characters of Lady Wisdom and Lady Folly are created for men and women to learn from. They warn us of the destruction folly can bring and urge us to live with wisdom and discretion, leading to a blessed (but not easy) and fulfilling life. God lets us choose what kind of life we are going to live. We have two voices we can listen to and two paths we can take: the voice of the world or the voice of God, the path of foolishness or the path of wisdom. God gives us a choice, and the quality of our lives depends on it. What kind of woman do you want to be, and what kind of life do you want to live?

Reflect

Think of some wise women you know. What sets their lives apart, and how does their character inspire you?

_____

_____

_____

_____

How would Lady Wisdom and Lady Folly use and show up on social media?

What area of your life do you need wisdom in?

Pray

God, help me to live with wisdom and become a woman of virtue and character. Teach me to live with discretion. Protect me from a life of foolishness and self-destruction as I seek to walk the narrow road that leads to life and peace.

Act

Write a verse from Proverbs about wisdom, such as Proverbs 8:11, and put it somewhere you will see daily to help you memorize it.

DAY 13

A HEALTHY BRAIN AND A SOUND MIND

The ultimate freedom we have as human beings is the power to select what we will allow or require our minds to dwell upon.
DALLAS WILLARD, RENOVATION OF THE HEART

If we want to flourish in body, mind, and spirit, we must care for our brains and master our thoughts. The brain is the physical, biological organ within a skull, composed of neurons and other cells that process and transmit information through electrical and chemical signals.[1] The mind, on the other hand, refers to the abstract, nonphysical realm of thoughts, emotions, consciousness, and cognitive processes.[2] There is a powerful interplay between the two. The brain's structure and functioning influence the experiences and state of our mind, and our mental state and thoughts also influence the brain's activity and even its physical structure.[3]

Science has proven what God tells us: we can be transformed by the renewing of our minds (see Romans 12:2). Our thoughts can physiologically change the structure of our brains. This is known as neuroplasticity, which is the brain's ability to form new neural pathways that can reshape our thoughts, behaviors, overall mental health, and well-being.

Dr. Daniel Amen, a renowned psychiatrist who teaches a holistic and comprehensive view of mental health, says, "You are not stuck with the brain you have."[4] In order to have healthy thoughts, you need to have a healthy brain. Positive thoughts and a healthy lifestyle improve the state of your brain. Social media overuse, stress, a poor diet, and a lack of exercise are some of the things that can make your brain unwell, which negatively impacts your mental health. We can't have good mental health if we don't care for our brains.

The fact that our brains can become healthier and function better and that we can change our thoughts is incredible news for our well-being. Friend, if you are battling depression, anxiety, and negative intrusive thoughts, there is so much hope for you.

Henry David Thoreau said, "Thought is the sculpture that can create the person you want to be." If you want to know who you are becoming, know the thoughts you think: "As he thinks in his heart, so is he" (Proverbs 23:7, NKJV). Our thoughts influence our beliefs, impacting our decisions and behaviors, which affects the quality of our lives. We become what we think about ourselves.

The use of social media causes us to have many thoughts that are often critical of ourselves, which we wouldn't otherwise have if we weren't using it. We must become aware of the thoughts we think because they will shape our mental frame of mind and how we see ourselves.

Mental health issues like anxiety and depression are the result of complex factors. Sometimes, the war waging in our minds is caused by a brain that is unwell because of different reasons such as head trauma, lack of sleep, drug and alcohol use, toxins, or other reasons. Sometimes it is not optimally functioning because of other factors such as chemical imbalances, and medical treatment such as medication is needed. Sometimes, this struggle is caused by our own untrue thoughts that are influenced by life experiences, trauma, false beliefs, and outside messages and content to which we expose ourselves. Other times, we are mentally and spiritually assaulted by Satan, whom the Bible calls the "father of lies" (John 8:44). Usually, a combination of physiological, lifestyle, environmental, and spiritual forces at play causes poor mental health.

Our negative thoughts and beliefs can become spiritual minefields that destroy us. The battles we face, whether it's depression, an eating disorder, trauma, insecurity, unworthiness, or anxiety, are won or lost in our minds. But if we can master our thoughts and become mentally fit, we can live victorious and flourishing lives.

We must be gatekeepers of our minds and decide which thoughts stay and which go. Philippians 4:8 says, "Finally, brothers and sisters, whatever is true, whatever is noble, whatever is right, whatever is pure, whatever is lovely, whatever is admirable—if anything is excellent or praiseworthy—think about such things." Mental fitness is like a muscle; it takes daily exercise and discipline to strengthen it. The more we train our minds to dwell on good, lovely, and true things, the more automatic these life-giving thoughts become.

We can be transformed by the renewing of our minds.

There are practical steps you can take to change your thoughts. The first step is to catch the negative thoughts and see if it is a spiritual assault on your mind: "Be alert and of sober mind. Your enemy the devil prowls around like a roaring lion looking for someone to devour" (1 Peter 5:8). Once you catch the thought, the next step is to take it captive so it cannot continue to speak lies over you: "We take captive every thought to make it obedient to Christ" (2 Corinthians 10:5). Then you can replace the lie with truth, but in order to do so you must have a word, verse, or truth declaration to replace that negative thought: "You will know the truth, and the truth will set you free" (John 8:32). The last step is to repeat that truth, verse, or truth declaration over and over. So the process goes like this: catch, take captive, replace, repeat.

If you are doing everything you can to overcome the negative thoughts in your mind and care for your brain, such as limiting social media use and developing life-giving habits, and you are still experiencing serious mental health struggles, it's time to look for outside professional help. Be encouraged that by caring for your brain, living a healthy lifestyle, and mastering your thoughts, your life and mental health can improve, and you can thrive in body, mind, and spirit.

Reflect

List the top three negative thoughts you have throughout your day.

_____

_____

_____

Open your Bible and write down truth statements or verses for each of these thoughts.

_____

_____

_____

List some ways you can begin replacing negative beliefs you have about yourself with truth.

_____

_____

_____

Pray

Empower me to transform my mind by changing my thoughts and caring for my brain. Teach me to meditate on Your promises and the good gifts in this life. Heal my mind from depression, anxiety, limiting beliefs, trauma, and worry. Make my brain healthy and my mind strong so I can live a victorious life.

Act

Write down a negative thought you regularly have. The next time it happens, follow this process and write it down here.

_____

_____

    Catch _____

    Take Captive _____

    Replace _____

    Repeat _____

DAY 14

SHOWING UP AS YOUR TRUE SELF

Are not two sparrows sold for a penny? Yet not one of them will fall to the ground outside your Father's care. And even the very hairs of your head are all numbered. So don't be afraid; you are worth more than many sparrows.

MATTHEW 10:29-31

There are two postures from which we can show up in the world. One posture asks, *Am I enough? Am I loved? Am I okay?* The other posture affirms that we are enough, we are loved, and we are okay. When we live from a posture of insecurity, we shrink back, hide, and dismiss our inherent value. Do you ever feel like you're too much or not enough? I assure you you're not, and know that this feeling is a common plight among women.

Childhood wounds, cultural messages, trauma, and abuse can leave an indelible mark that tells us our true selves are not acceptable or good enough. We can cope with this hurtful belief through people-pleasing, becoming addicted to harmful substances or activities, overachieving, hiding, self-destructing, numbing, and acting out a false version of ourselves that we think others on social media or in our lives will find more acceptable. As we do, we become disconnected from our true selves or who we are in God.

How are you showing up in this world? Are you playing small to win human approval so that others don't feel inferior or get upset with you? Are you allowing other people to determine your worth, or are you showing up unapologetically as your true self? Are you honoring your voice, wants, and needs?

It is a widespread pattern among women to put others first at the expense of being their authentic selves. We can misinterpret the verse that tells us to "die to ourselves" to think that we should always put our needs, wants, and opinions aside to serve others. But we should never do this at the expense of our dignity, allow others to take advantage of us, or deny our boundaries, wants, needs, and opinions.

One stressor of social media can come from managing an online persona, creating a false version of ourselves we think will win others over. But living for human approval is a recipe for emotional strife and unhappiness. When we hide behind people-pleasing, we hide who we've been made to be. This posture of false humility is often positively reinforced in our culture.

What would the world look like with you fully alive on a mission?

We can also be tempted to take on the drama and responsibilities of other people that are not ours to take on. This is not healthy empathy but codependency. Codependency is a pattern of relating in which you focus so much on other people that you become disconnected from your true self.[1] It is an epidemic among girls and women and is a form of self-betrayal.

Sometimes, when we want to be accepted, we become invisible so other people won't be intimidated by or upset with us. We play small. We don't speak up. We shrink back so we don't cause ripples or be a bother. But we lose our sense of self as we do. This pattern of diminishing our true selves can lead to resentment, depression, and exhaustion. It robs us of the strength God has instilled in us and keeps us from living out our purpose.

When we live from a posture of confidence in who God says we are, we change the world, set others free, and become fully alive. Jesus paid a high price for us. He didn't give His life for us so that we would play it safe. He has given us victory, a spirit of power and love, and a sound mind (see 2 Timothy 1:7). He has called us to live courageously. To become our true selves, we must walk in our identity as overcomers, image-bearers, and torch-carriers of the only hope this world has.

As His child, God created you to be strong, confident, and secure in His love for you. He created you to be powerful, victorious, self-assured, and courageous. If you've surrendered your life to God, this is the identity He gave you as His daughter—this is who you already are, whether you feel it or not. God does not want you to shrink back in insecurity. He wants you to take your place in the world with your chin up and shoulders back. He not only wants you to take up space in this world, but He wants you to show up unapologetically as your fully alive and confident self. When you shine, He shines.

Our dignity as women has been attacked since the beginning of time. Those who do not want to see us walk in strength, freedom, and confidence are afraid of us taking our place in this world because they know how powerful we can be. They will do anything or use anyone to keep us small. In the Gospels, we see how Jesus treated women. He gave them a voice, stood up for them, empowered them, radically loved them, and did not shame them. He forgave them and called them to step into their true selves and a better future. We can extend Jesus' example of how He treated women to the way we treat ourselves. It's time we learn how to stand our ground and not allow others to mistreat us. We honor our worth when we stand up for our dignity through words, actions, and boundaries.

God calls us to be humble and kind and to serve. But He doesn't call us to be these things at the expense of our dignity. We have been created to do hard and holy things: to fight against injustice, to protect our loved ones, to stand up for truth, to heal the brokenhearted, and to overcome evil with good. Our spiritual enemy wins when women stay small.

How would you show up in this world if you stopped comparing, shrinking, and dimming the light of Christ in you? What would you share, post, or comment on social media? What would the world look like with you fully alive on a mission? God wants to see you live fully alive in Him so He can be most glorified in your life. The Kingdom of God comes to earth when we take our place as the women we're made to be. Becoming your true self and having a strong sense of who you are requires believing you have a purpose and are valuable, and no one can take your place in this world. What would your life look like if you bravely stepped into the unshakable identity you've been given?

Reflect

Write down any times you have played small and put your needs aside.

_____
_____
_____
_____

Reflect on the definition of codependency. Is this a pattern in your life?

_____
_____
_____

What would your life look like if you died to insecurity and shame and started living into your identity?

_____
_____
_____
_____

Pray

God, teach me how to step into my authentic self in You. Empower me to honor my dignity and worth and live securely in who I am. Help me show up in this world confidently and live courageously, fully alive as the woman You created me to be.

Act

Write down five things you like about yourself. Practice self-assertiveness this week by gracefully expressing one of your needs, wants, or desires.

_____

_____

_____

_____

DAY 15

YOU ARE NOT AN IMPOSTER

No one can make you feel inferior without your consent.
ELEANOR ROOSEVELT

Do you ever feel like a fraud or a fake in your own life despite your accomplishments and talents? Do you dismiss your successes and strengths and attribute them to pure luck? These are the marks of imposter syndrome, which refers to a psychological phenomenon where individuals question their abilities and have a persistent fear of being revealed to be a fraud, despite their clear competence. "Individuals experiencing imposter syndrome often attribute their successes to luck or external factors, disregarding their own competence. This . . . can lead to anxiety, fear of exposure, and a cycle of overworking to prove oneself."[1]

We lose when we shrink back and play small in insecurity. Focusing on our shortcomings and failing to see our strengths or acknowledge our accomplishments paralyzes us from the life we've been made for. We can compare our lives to others on social media and feel we come up short. Dismissing your gifts can seem humble, but it is a false humility that rejects the *Imago Dei* or likeness of God that is built into your DNA as His child.

Believing the lie that you are not good enough is a stubborn refusal to receive your inherent worth. When we don't walk confidently in who we're created to be, it hinders our ability to pursue the extraordinary things God is doing with our lives. God has given you power and has handed you the keys to a life of greatness. Jesus affirms your identity: "You are the light of the world. A town built on a hill cannot be hidden. Neither do people light a lamp and put it under a bowl. Instead they put it on its stand, and it gives light to everyone in the house. In the same way, let your light shine before others, that they may see your good deeds and glorify your Father in heaven" (Matthew 5:14-16). You have been made to shine.

Dimming your light and believing you are an imposter doesn't just impact you; it impacts others. One of your purposes is to guide those in darkness toward light. Hiding your light does the world no good; it robs others of hope. It hinders them from stepping into their full potential and being spiritually transformed. Your light is to be revealed to the world, not concealed.

> Like every wildflower seed, you have untapped splendor and strength.

A refusal to believe your worth and potential is to deny the goodness of God's creation, a denial of the inherent value He gave you before you were born. You are God's handiwork, the apple of His eye, and the crown of all He has created. He knew you before He formed you. He has numbered the hairs on your head and written all your days in His book before one of them came to be. God looks at you and sees a masterpiece, a work of art with a unique design and purpose. You are not an imposter; you are a child of God who has been chosen before the foundation of the world, and no one can live your life but you.

You have not been made to exist; you've been made to live fully alive. Hidden within you is the potential for greatness. I buy over a thousand wildflower seeds every winter to sprinkle throughout my front- and backyard. Each latent seed teems with the potential to bloom with splendor into a Shasta daisy, snapdragon, California poppy, or dozens of other flowers. After scattering handfuls of them on the barren dirt, I close my eyes and try to envision what my yard will look like in three months after spring showers. When the plants timidly begin to surface from the soil, I am surprised by how few seeds have burst into life. How many of us are like those dormant seeds with unmet potential? We've been created to bloom, but self-doubt and limiting beliefs can prevent us from becoming all we're created to be. Like every wildflower seed, you have untapped splendor and strength in Him.

Your potential is limited only by the way you see yourself. The lies we believe about ourselves can result in a mediocre or broken life. We become what we think of ourselves. If we think we're a mess, our lives will be messy. If we think our value depends on the opinions of others, we'll always be chasing that next follow or like. If we think we're screw-ups, we'll self-destruct. If we think we're not good enough, we'll lead lives we feel aren't worthy.

The only way you can break free from insecurity is to receive and believe the true things God says about you. First, you must identify the lies and their roots so you can overcome them with truth. We can't maximize our potential, achieve our dreams, or live abundantly if we don't know our true identity.

You can't experience a breakthrough in your life if you stay stuck in insecurity and self-doubt. You have more gifts, power, strength, and potential than you will ever know. Who could you become if fear, insecurity, and poor self-worth were removed from your life? What would your life look like if you claimed your identity as a powerful, loved, original, and victorious woman? If you became fully alive? It's time to put your self-doubts aside and courageously step into your full potential. You're not an imposter. You're the real deal, and we need the real you.

Reflect

What lies are holding you back from stepping into your full potential?

_____

_____

_____

SOCIAL MEDIA RESET

What would you try to accomplish with your life if you could not fail?

_____

_____

_____

Close your eyes and envision the fully alive version of yourself. Now, describe what she is like and how she shows up in the world.

_____

_____

_____

Pray

God, help me overcome the lies I believe about myself so I can become the fully alive woman You created me to be. Show me what is possible and do more than I can ask, dream, or imagine in my life. I surrender my self-doubt and choose to walk in the truth of who You say I am as Your beloved child.

Act

Write down one action you can take to begin reaching an unfulfilled dream.

_____

_____

_____

DAY 16

BREAKING UP WITH YOUR IDEAL SELF

Let's just go ahead and be what we were made to be, without enviously or pridefully comparing ourselves with each other, or trying to be something we aren't.

ROMANS 12:6, MSG

Many of us have fashioned what we think is a better, more ideal version of our lives and ourselves on and off social media. The word *ideal* can be defined as "an idea or standard that seems perfect, and worth trying to achieve or obtain"[1] and "a standard of perfection, beauty, or excellence; of, relating to, or embodying an ideal."[2]

Our ideal self is characterized by the unique qualities we hold in high esteem, such as beauty, wealth, athleticism, style, intellectualism, charisma, and success. Each of us has different values, shaping the unattainable mental picture of our ideal self and life. While having big goals and an inspiring picture for your life can motivate you and lead to extraordinary success, it can also come with exhaustion and discontentment.

Perfection is praised in our culture and rewarded with fame and fortune on and off social media, but the pursuit of perfection will never satisfy our souls. We will never attain it here on earth. We crave perfection in this broken world, but we will only find it in heaven. Even if it seems we catch perfection for a minute, it will soon be gone. Having an ideal self is illusory, unrealistic, and unattainable. The gap between our real selves in person and the ideal selves we present online or in our actual lives creates a stifling tension that leads to anxiety and insecurity.

One of the dangers of having an ideal self is that she robs us of contentment in the present and overlooks our divine worth just as we are. She makes us feel as though we are never good enough and that we haven't yet arrived. We can exhaust our lives hustling to be perfect tomorrow when tomorrow may never come and perfection is impossible. All you have is today, and who you are in this moment is enough.

We might think that by becoming our ideal self, we will win human approval, but our perfect self actually separates us from others. Our authenticity, shortcomings, and even brokenness are a bridge to the people who love us for who we really are—people who deserve to journey through life with us. Our true self invites people to know and love us at our best and worst, fostering genuine connection, community, and a sense of belonging.

The world needs the real you, not the ideal you.

Think of a woman on social media who you perceive to have the perfect life and image. What emotions do you experience after scrolling through the highlight reel of her life? Are you inspired? Deflated? Happy? Envious? We usually don't feel great about ourselves in the presence of seemingly perfect people.

As women, our ideal self is often rooted in our physical appearance. It is natural for us to aspire toward unrealistic beauty standards our culture sets that are constantly being redefined. Sadly, this pressure can cause so many women to develop an unhealthy obsession with dieting and changing our bodies. Social media exacerbates our focus on the physical beauty of others and ourselves.

On social media, every time you pause to look at or like a photo of a woman who you perceive as beautiful and desirable, the algorithms will cause more photos of women like her to appear. Before you know it, your entire feed will be filled with the world's most beautiful women, making you feel like you'll never measure up. The more you see these photos, the more they can lead to increased body shame and even disordered eating. This is how social media can make eating disorders worse.[3]

When our own self-image consumes us, it prevents us from fully and beautifully bearing God's image to the world. The more we obsess over trying to meet ideal beauty standards, the more insecure and empty we will become. We have not been designed to be overly self-focused but to live a life bigger than ourselves, which truly restores our souls.

There is a difference between your ideal self and your authentic self. Your ideal self is who you think you should be. Your authentic self is who God has created you to be. Your ideal self is focused on the outward and physical—your looks, accomplishments, status, and wealth. Your authentic self is focused on the internal and everlasting—your character, values, dreams, personality, and faith. Your ideal self is shaped by who culture tells you to be, but your authentic self is who you were uniquely created to be.

Strife is the human soul's endless search for worthiness. Pursuing our ideal self causes strife, but embracing our authentic self brings our souls peace. When you break up with your ideal self, you become even more beautiful, real, and attractive to others. Your authentic self is more beautiful and lovable than your ideal self will ever be. The world needs the real you, not the ideal you: your authentic self, not your ideal self.

Reflect

Describe your ideal self. What does she look like? What does she do?

_____

_____

_____

Reflect on your authentic self. Who has God created you to be?

_____

_____

_____

How can you find satisfaction in being your authentic self and let go of any perfectionistic standards you may have for yourself?

Pray

Help me to relinquish the image I have of my ideal self and embrace who You created me to be. Thank You that You love me as I am and don't want perfection from me; You want my heart. Help me to find rest in You and beautifully bear Your image to the world.

Act

Think about one thing you have been doing to try to become your ideal self and surrender it to God.

DAY 17

GRIEVING BROKEN DREAMS

*Leave the broken, irreversible past in His hands, and
step out into the invincible future with Him.*
OSWALD CHAMBERS, MY UTMOST FOR HIS HIGHEST

Social media can be a daily reminder of broken dreams. We look at the extravagant wedding photos of that friend from high school and grieve the relationship we still don't have. We see the toned mom laughing as she holds her pigtailed little girl in her Pin-worthy kitchen. We see images of a happy family with perfect-looking children and parents blissfully in love. We envy our free-spirited friend who has backpacked through twenty-three countries.

What are your broken dreams? What are your unfulfilled desires? What do you look at on social media that reminds you of the things you want and don't have? God loves us and is a good Father who delights in giving good gifts, but He doesn't owe us anything.

None of us gets everything we want in life. None of us gets through this life unscathed. We all have disappointments. We all walk through suffering and hardship. I see wounds and broken dreams everywhere—in the gorgeous influencer whose mom passed away when she was nine, the girl with an eating disorder, the woman in her forties who is single without kids and longs for a family, the woman who was widowed in her thirties, the woman diagnosed with terminal cancer.

On social media, we see pretty smiles; we rarely see ugly tears. We see couples embracing; we don't see their fights or infidelities. We see women holding their perfect babies; we don't see their miscarriages, postpartum depression, or sleepless nights. We see a woman's perfect body; we don't see her binging and purging.

What do you long for? What do you want more than anything? What are you pleading for from God? If needed, allow yourself permission to grieve the life that wasn't yours to live. Ask God to help you praise Him for what is rather than dwell on what could have been. God might not answer every prayer or give you everything you want in life, but He showers us with undeserved blessings. Some of these gifts get overlooked or remain wrapped because we exhaust our mental energy by focusing on the ones we didn't receive, dismissing all the good and lovely things we have been given.

God can handle your emotions.

Psalm 37:4 says, "Delight yourself in the Lord, and he will give you the desires of your heart" (ESV). We might interpret this verse as God giving us everything we want, like that relationship, baby, opportunity, or material possession. But the promise of Scripture is that as we delight in God, our hearts will find peace and contentment. As we find our satisfaction by abiding in God, we will find joy; our souls will be at rest even if we have broken dreams or unfulfilled desires. Our hearts will change when we seek God's Kingdom, not ours. Our overriding desires will not be so much for material things, status, or relationships but for the eternal things of God, which this world will never provide.

God can handle your emotions. It's okay to be sad. Allow yourself to grieve your broken dreams and mourn the unfulfilled longings of your heart. Let your tears fall unashamedly. Clench your fists and yell in anger if you must.

Sometimes, we will grieve our broken dreams or unmet desires for the rest of our lives. People will impose their plans for your life on you, and you will make your own plans, but only God's plan for your life will transpire: "Many are the plans in a person's heart, but it is the Lord's purpose that prevails" (Proverbs 19:21).

Trust that His plan for your life is best, even if suffering, sickness, and heartache come with it. Amid grief, we can have hope that in heaven, all our tears will be wiped away, and every hard thing will be redeemed. Sometimes, unfulfilled dreams make other good dreams possible. What does your unfulfilled desire make possible? What kind of life does your singleness or childlessness enable? What does your breakup or the rejection from your college or dream job allow you to do instead?

Delighting ourselves in the Lord requires us to turn our focus away from what we don't have and be grateful for what we do. Instead of comparing our lives to others on and off social media, we must focus on all that is good, lovely, pure, and praiseworthy and rejoice in the gifts we've been given. We'll stay stuck if all we dwell on is our unfulfilled desires, and we won't be able to move on to even better things.

In time, God will mend your broken heart when you give Him all the pieces. Lay your broken dreams and unmet desires at His feet. Let yourself grieve and weep. Then, when you're ready, wipe your tears, rise to a new day, marvel at the miracle of your life, and embrace the beautiful story that is yours to live. Praise God for every good and perfect gift from above. Trust in His plans for you. Embrace your one and only life. Release your dreams and accept God's dream for you.

Reflect

What are some of your broken dreams or unfulfilled longings?

_____

_____

_____

_____

_____

What are you grieving?

_____
_____
_____

What does your life make possible?

_____
_____
_____

Pray

Dear God, thank You for the gift of my life and every good and perfect gift You have given me. I surrender my plan for my life and trust that Yours is better. Heal my wounded heart and comfort me in my disappointment and grief. Give me peace and joy as I delight in You, and teach me to embrace the beautiful life You have given me.

Act

Write down three good gifts God has given you.

_____
_____
_____

DAY 18

ALL THE FEELINGS

LORD, you are the God who saves me; day and night I cry out to you. May my prayer come before you; turn your ear to my cry.

PSALM 88:1-2

In order to live a flourishing life, we must learn to manage our emotions in a healthy way. Struggles such as the death of a loved one, the loss of a dream, a breakup, or a health issue can be extremely painful and hard. These experiences can leave us with difficult emotions, which make it easy to turn to unhealthy coping mechanisms. Our responses to the difficulties of life and the emotions and trauma we experience are critical.

If we choose to numb emotions like anger, sadness, shame, and fear with endless scrolling or another escape, we will be mentally, physically, and spiritually unwell. Emotions are data that tell us about our needs and desires. Our thoughts, experiences, beliefs, and the way we interpret events influence our emotions, which in turn influence our decision-making and behavior.

As women, we can be used to thinking that emotions like anger are bad and that we must suppress them, but God wants us to be honest with every emotion we feel and bring it to Him. The book of Psalms is filled with prayers that express every emotion a person can have, including happiness, sadness, fear, anger, love, joy, anxiety, guilt, shame, envy, jealousy, and excitement.

Psalms is the book of honest emotions. There is even a category in it known as psalms of lament, which comprises one-third of the book. These honest prayers teach us that crying out to God is okay. He hears us in our heartache and pain and does not turn a deaf ear. When you don't know how to cope with what you feel, let the prayers in the psalms be your prayers; let those words be your words. When you feel downcast, betrayed, alone, angry, or abandoned, cry out to God in honesty without holding back your emotions. When you don't know what to do or where to turn, yell, feel, hide your face in this book, and cry unashamedly until its pages are stained with your tears.

> God loves you the same in your gladness and sadness.

We can either cope with difficult emotions in healthy or harmful ways. When a painful emotion surfaces, it can be natural to react impulsively by escaping it through self-destructive behaviors. When these feelings surface, we must resist impulsivity and bravely face them. We can tend to cope with challenging emotions through the escape of our choice, like overusing social media.

These destructive behaviors can offer us a tempting reprieve from reality and the difficulties of life, but they can come with dangerous consequences. These unhealthy coping mechanisms can give us temporary relief and distract us from painful emotions, but they cause more distress in the long run.

When we draw near to God and face our difficult emotions, we can walk by the Spirit in wholeness and freedom and not gratify the desires of our flesh through escaping in harmful ways (see Galatians 5:16). Scripture tells us, "For the flesh desires what is contrary to the Spirit, and the Spirit what is contrary to the flesh. They are in conflict with each other, so that you are not to do whatever you want" (Galatians 5:17).

The Holy Spirit is our wise and loving Counselor who gives us peace that surpasses all understanding and comforts our troubled hearts. He even prays on our behalf when we don't have the words to express our emotions: "The Spirit helps us in our weakness. We do not know what we ought to pray for, but the Spirit himself intercedes for us" (Romans 8:26).

Managing difficult emotions in a healthy way is crucial for well-being and happiness. We can manage our emotions by acknowledging and naming them and feeling them without shame. Praying to God, reading Scripture, talking to friends, seeing a counselor, breathing deeply, exercising, making healthy lifestyle choices, journaling, doing activities we love, and finding a safe space to talk are some beneficial ways to process our grief, hurts, and trauma.

The acronym HALT (Hungry, Angry, Lonely, Tired) can also encourage us to check in with ourselves and be a helpful tool for gaining awareness of our physical, emotional, and mental states. Asking ourselves if we are hungry, angry, lonely, and tired before making a decision can help us take care of ourselves, meet our needs, and manage our emotions in healthy ways.

Ask God to comfort you and give you the courage to sit with your feelings without numbing them. Give yourself permission to experience emotions you have been told are bad, and believe that God loves you the same in your gladness and sadness.

Be encouraged—you can bravely face all of your feelings and learn to cope with them in healthy ways. Run to God boldly, unashamedly. Do not hide or pretend or stuff. Do not run away or numb. God loves you—all of you. You will never be too much or not enough for Him. Come to Him, and He will restore your soul and give you peace.

Reflect

What difficult emotions do you feel?

_____

_____

_____

_____

What do you think causes these emotions?

_____
_____
_____

How do you cope with them?

_____
_____
_____

Pray

God, thank You for allowing me to be honest with You. Thank You for welcoming all of my emotions and wanting me to run to You for comfort and relief. Help me resist the temptation to escape through unhealthy and destructive behaviors. Thank You for loving all of me and telling me that I will never be too much for You.

Act

List three difficult emotions you experienced this past week. Write down a few healthy ways you can cope with them.

_____
_____
_____

DAY 19

HEALING FROM SHAME

*Goodness and beauty can prevail in the
face of overwhelming shame.*

CURT THOMPSON, *THE SOUL OF SHAME*

Shame is a complex emotion that keeps women from stepping into our identity and purpose. Curt Thompson, the author of *The Soul of Shame*, explains, "Researchers have described *shame* as a feeling that is deeply associated with a person's sense of self, apart from any interactions with others; *guilt*, on the other hand, emerges as a result of something I have done that negatively affects someone else. Guilt is something I feel because I have *done* something bad. Shame is something I feel because I *am* bad."[1]

Shame prevents us from having a healthy sense of self. It keeps us from fully showing up in this world as God's dearly loved image-bearers. It paralyzes us and can lead to an unfulfilling life. Shame can become a suffocating experience that shapes every thought we have and action we take. It is often associated with mental health issues, but it is also felt universally. Shame is an epidemic and pervasive part of the human experience, but it's not the identity we've been designed to live into.

Seemingly perfect images on social media can make us feel like we will never be good enough. Identifying the sources of our shame and getting help for them can help us heal and walk in our God-given worth.

Much of our shame comes from comparing ourselves to others. Social media is a playground for shame. It offers daily reminders that we're not good, skinny, beautiful, popular, or successful enough. When we post photos and videos of ourselves on social media, we can often feel exposed and vulnerable to others' judgments.

I hope that during your respite from social media, you are experiencing more joy and contentment as you compare yourself less and wake up to the beauty and wonder of your own life. I hope this journey is helping you turn away from the people and things that make you feel less than. I hope that instead of looking to others for validation, you are looking up to God, who is the source of your worth. If you choose to reenter social media after this reset, ask God to help you show up authentically, stop comparing, and not seek approval from others.

Shame is not your identity. Daughter is.

Satan is the master shame artist; Jesus is the lifter of our shame. The Gospels show how our hero, Jesus, erased shame among the women He encountered. He intervened before a woman who was caught cheating on her husband was stoned to death. He swooped down, embraced her with His love, forgave her, and invited her into a better life (see John 8:1-11). He healed the woman who had been bleeding for twelve years and was likely forced to live alone, away from society. He exchanged the name "outcast" for "daughter," giving her a brand-new identity (see Luke 8:43-48). He delighted in the sinful woman who anointed his feet with expensive perfume as a legalistic, religious man condemned her for doing so (see Luke 7:36-39).

Shame can lead us to withdraw from others and isolate ourselves because we fear rejection. Withdrawing reinforces shame because it thrives in isolation. Hiding keeps us from healing and prevents others from being blessed by our presence in their lives.

Brennan Manning said, "If we conceal our wounds out of fear and shame, our inner darkness can neither be illuminated nor become a light for others."[2] When you share your struggles with kindhearted people who care for you, shame lessens because you realize that you're not alone. Your struggles should only be shared in safe places and with the right people. Sharing with the wrong people or with people publicly, like on social media, can leave you exposed and vulnerable to harmful comments that can increase your shame.

Looking to God and away from the world brings light to our souls. Psalm 34:5 says, "Those who look to him are radiant; their faces are never covered with shame." In my book *Wonderfully Made*, I remind readers, "When we take off our old selves or who we've been apart from God and clothe ourselves in our new identity, shame dissipates and we rise to live in freedom and radiance. A radiant woman looks up to God for her worth, rather than to herself or others."[3]

What is the "shame story" of your life? Jesus stands ready to erase it and write you a new story: a story of love, worth, and belonging. Imagine confidently showing up in the world, secure and sure of yourself. Envision what your life could look like if you really believed your worth. When you know Jesus and know your value, it changes everything. Shame is not your identity. Daughter is.

Reflect

In what areas of your life do you experience shame?

___

___

___

What do you think are the origins and causes of your shame?

___

___

What can you do to walk more confidently in your God-given worth?

Pray

God, thank You for coming to heal me from shame and giving me an unshakable identity as Your beloved daughter. Teach me to look away from the world and others for my worth and turn to You. Lift my shame and make me radiant.

Act

Write a verse or truth declaration to memorize that you can say when you feel shame.

DAY 20

FINDING YOUR PEOPLE

*Let us consider how to stir up one another to love and
good works, not neglecting to meet together, as is the
habit of some, but encouraging one another.*

HEBREWS 10:24-25, ESV

Do you experience loneliness? College was the loneliest time in my life. Even though I was surrounded by people, I felt like no one knew me. My loneliness led to heightened depression, which led me to isolate and feel even more disconnected from people. Due to the rise of social media, we live in the most connected yet isolated and lonely time history has ever seen. We are facing an epidemic of loneliness marked by widespread feelings of disconnectedness and social isolation. Over half, or 52 percent, of Americans report feeling lonely.[1] Gen Z, which is comprised of people born between 1997 and 2012, is known to be the loneliest generation in all of history, with 73 percent reporting feeling alone sometimes or always.[2]

While social media makes it possible for us to connect with almost anyone in the world, it has come at the cost of true connection, which we can only find through face-to-face interactions and real-life relationships. A core definition of *community* is "all the people who live in a particular area, country, etc."[3] Before the industrial and technological revolutions, communities comprised men, women, and children who lived near one another and had tight-knit relationships in smaller social circles. They regularly conversed, gathered, and experienced life with one another.

Today, neighbors rarely talk to each other, people keep to themselves, and many people spend more time with their phones than with other people. Our society praises individualism. Fractured families are common, and many live far away from loved ones. We can settle for inauthentic and surface-level online connections and superficial communication, often through DMs, likes, and three-word text messages next to smiling heart emojis. Now, more than ever, it is easy to feel alone and left out when we see posts on social media of friends getting together without us, especially when we weren't invited. After spending time on social media, do you feel more connected to people or more isolated?

Our digital hyperconnectivity can make us feel fragmented and like no one really knows us. The average Facebook user has 338 friends.[4] Over half of Instagram users have more than one thousand followers.[5] We weren't designed to know the daily ins and outs of hundreds or thousands of people. We only have the emotional capacity for a small number of close and meaningful friendships. Relationship experts hold that having three to six friends is the "'sweet spot' for reaping the happiness benefits of friendship."[6] You'll be happier with a few real friends than you will with thousands of followers.

Shame can drive us to isolate. We fear if people really knew us, they wouldn't accept us. We risk getting hurt or being rejected when we engage in relationships. People will let us down, and we will let them down. In spite of this, community, love, and friendship are always worth the risk. We must trust that even if people let us down, God will not, and He will be faithful to heal any relational wounds we might experience. Your friendship and love can make someone else's life better. By being in a relationship with them, you can change their life.

We cannot sit idly by and expect friendship, love, and community to happen to us. Breaking free from loneliness requires prayer, effort, intentionality, and action. We can wallow in self-pity for feeling lonely or choose to intentionally seek out community. It is scary to put ourselves out there—to start a conversation with a stranger, attend church alone, go on a date, join a club, or invite someone to coffee.

We all crave deep and fulfilling friendships, but it can be hard to find them. Dale Carnegie, author of the famous book *How to Win Friends and Influence People*, said, "You can make more friends in two months by becoming genuinely interested in other people than you can in two years by trying to get other people interested in you."[7]

Become the kind of friend you would like to have. Find emotionally healthy friends who share your values and interests and who you enjoy being with. Become a good listener and care for, serve, and encourage your friends. You have so much beauty and love to offer people, and you deserve healthy friendships and relationships that bring joy to your life. Your friendship will also bring joy to others.

You'll be happier with a few real friends than you will with thousands of followers.

Though it is full of broken people, just like everywhere, a good place to find community can be in a *healthy* church. Seek out people who love and follow God and want to love people the way He does. Research has found that people who regularly attend church services and events report lower levels of loneliness and more happiness.[8]

Social media is also an amazing way to meet new people and build relationships, but it is important to know that online friendships often lack depth and don't provide the deep connection we crave. After your reset, use social media intentionally to connect with positive, like-minded people, and try to foster those relationships offline as well.

It can be so unbearable to feel alone that we settle into unhealthy relationships. Ask God to give you wisdom and discernment in your relationships. Don't maintain harmful relationships with friends or romantic partners because you don't want to be alone. Doing so will only bring more emotional wounds. You will be far better off being single or with fewer friends than in a destructive relationship. Know your value, and do not settle for anyone who does not love you well.

Not only can you cultivate community and friendship for yourself, but you can also reach out to lonely people and give them a place to belong by showing them love and hospitality. Ask God to show you how to be a friend and bring you life-giving friends, relationships, and community.

If you want to have friends, you must be friendly. If you want community, you must go on a hunt to find it. If you want to find love, you must let your guard down. You have not been made to do life alone. You will begin to flourish and come alive in the presence of healthy, loving people when you seek them.

Reflect

On a scale of 0 to 10 (10 being extremely lonely), how lonely do you feel?

If you feel lonely or have a lack of meaningful relationships, why do you think this is?

Make a list of your closest friends or some people you would like to get to know better.

Pray

God, remove any loneliness I feel and replace it with community, friendships, and a sense of belonging. Bring people into my life who will love and accept me and make my life more meaningful. Give me courage and wisdom as I seek out community, love, and friendship.

Act

Put yourself out there. Invite someone to coffee, join people for dinner, participate in a book club or Bible study, go on a date, or volunteer for a cause you care about.

DAY 21

BEAUTY SECRETS

When a woman knows that she is loved and loved deeply, she glows from the inside. This radiance stems from a heart that has had its deepest questions answered. Am I lovely? Am I worth fighting for? Have I been and will I continue to be romanced? *When these questions are answered yes, a restful, quiet spirit settles in a woman's heart.*

JOHN AND STASI ELDREDGE, CAPTIVATING

Think of the girls and women you love to be around. How do they make you feel? What qualities do they have in common? I'm guessing it's not their clothing size or hairstyle, number of social media followers, height, or how they dress. I imagine they make you feel seen, valued, genuinely loved and that they care for you. I bet that when you are with them, they are fully present and take a genuine interest in you. They glow radiantly with light and joy. These are the women whose company you want to keep. They have everlasting beauty, as Proverbs 31:30 describes: "Charm is deceptive, and beauty is fleeting; but a woman who fears [loves and respects] the LORD is to be praised." Our world esteems physical beauty, but "The LORD does not look at the things people look at. People look at the outward appearance, but the LORD looks at the heart" (1 Samuel 16:7).

We might think our lives would be better or we would be happier if we met the world's beauty standards. Who doesn't want to look like a supermodel? The attention that comes with meeting these standards is desirable. We might believe it will bring us the love, attention, and approval we're searching for. However, even meeting these ever-changing ideals does not guarantee love, happiness, or a better life. Many of the world's most physically beautiful women, just like other women, struggle with mental health issues, broken relationships, addictions, and low self-worth and are far from living a happy life.

When we are overly self-focused and consumed by how we look, we aren't fully present in our lives and can miss out on living an abundant life of wholeness and freedom. As I wrote in my book *Wonderfully Made*, "Building our life on our outward appearance is like building a hillside mansion on shifting sand. Physical beauty cannot sustain the weight of our true worth."[1] When we obsess over physical beauty, we are worshiping something that will not last, something that will disappear. Focusing on appearance and spending our lives striving to attain ideal beauty standards can keep us from fully living out our true purpose, which is to love God, enjoy our lives, and love others well.

> *True beauty is not fleeting but everlasting.*

But when we take God at His word and believe we have been beautifully and wonderfully created, we have a soul at rest and are free to make others feel valued and beautiful. The less we think about ourselves and our appearance, the more free we become. We are also no longer consumed with searching for validation on social media or in real life. The more we trust what God says about us, the more we have a heart at rest. The more we love others, the more beautiful we become.

What God esteems is always different than what the world values. Beauty is less about how you look and more about your character, faith, and how you make others feel. Scripture agrees: "Your beauty should not come from outward adornment, such as elaborate hairstyles and the wearing of gold jewelry or fine clothes. Rather, it should be that of your inner self, the unfading beauty of a gentle and quiet spirit, which is of great worth in God's sight" (1 Peter 3:3-4). This "gentle and quiet spirit" is about having a heart at rest that is hidden in God, and doesn't mean you have to tame your personality. True beauty glows deep from within a woman's soul. It is a beauty that is not fleeting but everlasting. It is a beauty that only grows with the passing of time.

One night before going out with friends, I found myself getting too hung up on my appearance. I sensed God say to me in the quietness of my heart, "Allie, it's not about how you look; it's about how you make others feel." I now repeat this when I'm getting ready, which helps me be present to others and focus on making them feel loved and valued. The less concerned we become with being found beautiful and the more concerned we become with loving others well, the happier, more free, and truly beautiful we become.

God's creation is not only good but stunning. You are God's image-bearer and the crown of creation—the finishing touch on all He has made. Can you think of a higher honor? It takes faith to believe this. But when you do, you will have a heart at rest—and believe you are beautiful, loved, and enough.

Even though inner beauty is what really matters, it is good to take pride in your appearance and present yourself in a way that makes you feel confident. God delights in you as His masterpiece and wants you to value yourself. He feels great about you, so why shouldn't you feel great about yourself?

Clothing, hairstyles, jewelry, and makeup are some ways in which you can express yourself and improve self-confidence. Treat yourself to clothes you like (but don't go into debt!), do your makeup if you want, and style your hair in a way you love. Wake up, take pride in your appearance, believe you are beautiful, and put your best face forward. It's important to feel good about yourself, and then it's time to start making other people feel good.

What kind of woman do you want to be? How do you want others to feel in your presence? God offers you a beauty that will never fade. It's a beauty that makes everyone in your presence feel valued. It's a beauty that will change the world.

Reflect

Write the names of women you love to be around who make you feel loved and valued. Think about what they have in common.

_____

_____

_____

How do you want others to feel when they are in your presence?

_____

_____

_____

When do you feel the most beautiful?

_____

_____

_____

Pray

Lord, make me a woman of unfading beauty who believes that I am beautifully and wonderfully made. Help me to love others and make them feel seen and known.

Act

Ask a friend to grab a coffee. The day you meet up with her, wear clothes and style yourself in a way that makes you feel confident. Then, focus on listening to and encouraging her during your time together.

DAY 22

MAKING PEACE WITH YOUR BODY

Do you not know that your bodies are temples of the Holy Spirit, who is in you, whom you have received from God? You are not your own.

1 CORINTHIANS 6:19

I came across a book title that made me laugh out loud: *Just When You're Comfortable in Your Own Skin, It Starts to Sag.* If you are given many years on this earth, one day, you'll have gray hair and many wrinkles, and your body will begin to break down. For those of us who spent our lives in body angst, we will realize our legacy is not measured by the size we wear but by the lives we lead. We'll face the truth that we are more than our bodies. We have an eternal soul in a body that will be renewed in heaven: "So we do not lose heart. Though our outer self is wasting away, our inner self is being renewed day by day" (2 Corinthians 4:16, ESV).

The media presents unrealistic beauty standards that are constantly being redefined, leading to stifling comparisons that make us feel like our bodies are not good enough. This can cause us to view our bodies as broken projects to be fixed and critiqued. One study found that young women who spend a lot of time on social media were more likely to compare their looks to other women and to "self-objectify."[1]

Self-objectification is something I've struggled with during years of poor body image, and I'm not alone. To self-objectify is to see yourself as a body first and a person second. It is so common among girls and women, much as a result of our culture. Self-objectifying behaviors can include but are not limited to frequent selfies, critiquing one's appearance, and comparing oneself to other women and images in the media. The danger with self-objectification is that compelling research has found that it is associated with a number of ills, including body shame, appearance anxiety, depression, and eating disorders.[2]

Your body is not a measure of your worth. It is not meant to be critiqued, abused, or disrespected. It has a sacred purpose: to glorify God, love others, and sustain our miraculous lives.

There are many fix-it tactics we might choose for our personal body projects: chronic dieting, overexercise, and plastic surgery. Whatever method or combination of methods we might choose has an associated opportunity cost—a life more meaningfully spent. Regardless of its shape, size, disabilities, or limb differences, your body is good, and God did not make a mistake when He created you. I'll say it again, friend—you are wonderfully made. On my mirror I wrote, "Your body is good. Now go love people." I remind myself I don't need to change my body; I just need to care for it.

> *Our legacy is not measured by the size we wear but by the lives we lead.*

There are things you can do to improve your body image, like practicing gratitude for what your body allows you to do. Your eyes allow you to soak in the beauty of creation all around you. Your arms allow you to hug the people you love the most. Your legs carry you through this world. Next time you express disdain for a certain part of your body, replace it with thoughts of gratitude for what your body allows you to do.

Shut out the toxic narrative of comparison and protect your eyes. Unfollow triggering accounts on social media, and be mindful of what movies you watch, the media you consume, and the time you spend on certain websites such as Pinterest. During your social media reset, are you feeling more comfortable in your body? Are you comparing yourself less? If you use social media after the reset, fill your feed with encouraging content and women who inspire you to improve your self-confidence.

Say no to comparison. It is natural to compare ourselves and our bodies to others, but we can break the habit. Every time I am tempted to compare myself to another woman, in my mind I say, *She is wonderfully made, and so am I. She is beautiful, and so am I. Her life is a miracle, and so is mine.* I then pray a blessing over her. Try doing this the next time you are tempted to compare. It will help you shift your mindset from comparison to celebration of God for the way He created you both.

Start living fully in your present body. Treasure, care for, and enjoy your body now, no matter your weight or appearance. Enjoy the emotional and physical benefits of exercise and find activities you enjoy. Even a short walk will make you feel better in your body. If you're struggling with food or body image issues, talk about them with safe people, and if you are having disordered eating behaviors, it's important to get help.

Skinny or thin doesn't mean healthy. Focus your efforts on being physically fit, well-nourished, and emotionally free rather than chasing the thin ideal. Instead of trying to change your body, learn to care for it. Optimal health comes in a diversity of shapes and sizes. Adopt better habits for your well-being rather than to look a certain way.

Imagine what your life could be like if you didn't experience body shame or exhaust your energy on trying to perfect yourself. Imagine the other ways you can spend your thoughts and time. Ask God to heal you from body shame. Pray Psalm 142:7: "Set me free from my prison, that I may praise your name." You are God's masterpiece designed to love people, delight in the gift of your life, and do a phenomenal amount of good in the world. When we begin to believe deep down in our souls that we are wonderfully and phenomenally made, taking God at His word, we become free and are able to live the life we're made for.

Reflect

How would your life be different if you believed your body was good?

What social media accounts or other types of media that you've been consuming are triggering body shame and would be beneficial to stop looking at?

How can you embrace the body you have now, and what is one kind thing you can do to show respect and gratitude for your body?

Pray

Thank You for the gift of my body. Make it an instrument of Your love and peace. Help me to believe that what You say about my body is good and true. Lord, show me the path to freedom.

Act

Engage in a physical activity that brings you joy and freedom this week.

DAY 23

HOW TO LIVE HAPPIER AND HEALTHIER

Rejoice in the Lord always. I will say it again: Rejoice!
PHILIPPIANS 4:4

Imagine waking up tomorrow and feeling better in your body, mind, and spirit than you ever have before. Picture yourself having endless energy, feeling great in your body, having mental clarity, liking who you are, and feeling joyful and excited. How would your life be different?

Our body, mind, and spirit have been intentionally designed to have a symbiotic relationship. An illness or physical health condition can affect our spiritual and mental well-being, causing distress. When our mental health suffers from stress, anxiety, and depression, it can weaken our immune system and crush our spirit and sense of purpose. When we don't have a firm spiritual grounding, we are more likely to experience mental and emotional distress, which can negatively impact our overall health. On the other hand, we experience optimal wellness when we are thriving in all three areas of our lives.

When we approach our well-being holistically, we recognize that in order to flourish, we must invest in these three aspects of our being. Neglecting our body, mind, or spirit can disrupt the other spheres and lead to issues in other areas.

HOW TO LIVE HAPPIER AND HEALTHIER

The good news is that we can live a happier and healthier life by implementing positive habits and stopping bad ones, making lifestyle changes, and establishing beneficial rhythms and routines. Hopefully, taking a break from social media has already been a positive change for you. I know this will only touch the surface, but I am going to share what I have found to be the top five practices to nurture each area of your life—your body, mind, and spirit, totaling fifteen tips to choose from to spur you on toward a vibrant life.

As you implement new habits in your daily life, hold yourself to a standard of grace, not perfection. Be gentle with yourself on this journey. It's about progress, not perfection. By practicing one or two of these habits, you can enhance your physical, emotional, and spiritual well-being and improve the quality of your life. You are worth it.

> Be gentle with yourself on this journey. It's about progress, not perfection.

First, let's tackle how to nurture your body. The most important thing you can do is get enough sleep. Sleep is essential to every function of your body, and you cannot be well without an adequate amount, which is at least seven hours a night.

Second, I know this isn't new information, but building upon this, exercising daily improves your mood, soothes anxiety and stress, strengthens your immune system, and helps you sleep and function better. It also boosts self-confidence and energy levels.

Third, drinking enough water is similarly essential for the function of your body and mind, physical performance, and skin health. Aim to follow the 8x8 rule, which is to drink eight 8-ounce glasses of water daily. This can vary depending on your physical activity and your body's needs.

Fourth, periodically having your blood work done can help detect health issues, monitor chronic conditions, and inform you of any lifestyle changes you need to make to optimize your health. Lastly, avoid alcohol and drugs and enjoy nourishing foods, including fruits and vegetables, nuts, seeds, and lean proteins. Allow yourself to enjoy treats and don't restrict foods, but try to limit your intake of processed foods with refined sugars that contain empty calories, causing inflammation and disease. You'll feel better, and your mind and body will thank you.

Now, I want to share some practical ways you can nurture your mind that have helped me overcome depression and thrive. Adequate sleep, exercise, and a nourishing diet, which we just discussed, are essential to the mind's well-being and your brain's health. Building upon these, the number one thing you can do to care for your mind is to transform your thoughts, which we discussed in-depth in "A Healthy Brain and a Sound Mind."

A second way to enhance your mental health is to manage your stress levels. Chronic stress has detrimental effects on your mental health. Practice stress-reducing activities such as deep breathing and exercise. Third, managing the inputs you allow into your life, including the consumption of news and media, can decrease your anxiety levels and improve your overall mental health. You are already doing this through your social media reset. Fourth, practice talking to yourself with kindness and compassion, remembering that the most important conversations you'll have during your day will be the ones you have with yourself and with God. Last, you can memorize verses, truth declarations, and affirmations that will rewire the neural pathways in your brain to transform your mind.

To nurture your spirit, the most transformative thing you can do is have daily quiet time. There is nothing more refreshing than starting your day off with prayer and reading God's Word. Psalm 90:14 says, "Satisfy us in the morning with your unfailing love, that we may sing for joy and be glad all our days." Second, make time for your passions. Studies have shown that when you are following your passions, you are decreasing your stress levels and increasing your happiness.[1]

Third, practice the Sabbath or take one day off a week to rest from your work and do restorative things for your soul. Fourth, go outside, play, and enjoy the wonder and beauty of creation. Last, seek out and engage in meaningful relationships. Surround yourself with people who are following God and moving in a good direction. Look for positive communities, such as church groups, to meet new people. Invest in these relationships offline and ask God to help you be the kind of friend you would like to have.

I know this is a quick crash course in wellness; however, I hope it is a starting point for you to learn to invest in your physical, mental, and spiritual well-being so that you can thrive and flourish in your life. I encourage you to make time to invest in your health and wellness. Be encouraged that through grit and God's grace, you can live a more vibrant, happier, and healthier life.

Reflect

Next to each area (body, mind, and spirit), list how you currently feel on the left and how you would like to feel on the right.

	How I currently feel	How I would like to feel
Body		
Mind		
Spirit		

Pray

God, help me make changes that will allow me to experience vibrant wellness in body, mind, and spirit. Help me to steward my health well with gratitude and responsibility. Heal and strengthen my physical, mental, and spiritual health so I can better live the life You created me for.

Act

Choose one of these fifteen wellness tips and commit to implementing it this week.

DAY 24

THE MEAN SISTERS

A cheerful heart is good medicine, but a crushed spirit dries up the bones.

PROVERBS 17:22

If you're like a lot of girls and women today, you might be getting bullied by one or two mean sisters—anxiety and depression. Anxiety, depression, and other mental health issues, such as eating disorders, have been rising dramatically over the past decade.[1] They are destroying and wreaking havoc on too many of our lives. While it's not the whole story, we can no longer deny the correlation between the rising mental health crisis and the onset and use of social media.[2] The good news is that we don't have to let these mean sisters shove us around, and we can win this catfight.

Anxiety is the most widespread mental health condition and affects forty million people in the United States, or 19 percent of the population. Women are 50 percent more likely to suffer from anxiety than men, and 31.9 percent of adolescents ages thirteen to eighteen are impacted by anxiety.[3] For some, anxiety can be more than just occasional nervousness or worry. People with anxiety disorders experience fear and worry that is excessive, continuous, and intense. It can make functioning in their daily lives difficult. Anxiety symptoms can include nausea, sweating, trembling, and a rapid heart rate. Clinical anxiety can make concentrating, talking, and focusing difficult and can cause feelings of restlessness and a sense of impending doom or danger. It can also result in sleep disturbances and lead us to avoid social situations or activities that might trigger anxiety, causing isolation and withdrawal, which makes it worse.[4]

Anxiety's fraternal twin sister is depression. Depression is the other most common and serious mental health condition that also bullies women more than men. It affects about 3.8 percent of the world's population and 5 percent of adults.[5] According to the Centers for Disease Control, three in five, or 57 percent of teen girls in the United States felt persistently sad or hopeless in 2021. This rate of depression is double that of boys and marks a 60 percent increase.[6] From 2010 to 2015, the rate of suicides among teen girls skyrocketed by 65 percent, correlating with the onset of smartphones and social media.[7]

You can thrive and lead a flourishing, wholehearted life.

Symptoms of clinical depression include persistent sadness or emptiness, loss of interest in previously enjoyable activities, changes in appetite or weight, sleep disturbances, fatigue, feelings of worthlessness, difficulty concentrating, irritability, and thoughts of death or suicide. Depression is damaging to every area of someone's life, including work, school, and relationships, making it difficult to do daily tasks and function. According to the World Health Organization, "depression is the leading cause of ill health and disability worldwide."[8] Suicide is the fourth leading cause of death for people ages fifteen to twenty-nine.[9]

There are many reasons why anxiety and depression mess with us, and it is different for each person. Both are a result of complex social, psychological, spiritual, and biological factors and are often a combination of all of these influences. Genetic predisposition, family history, brain chemistry, and lifestyle can cause or contribute to anxiety and depression. Personality traits like perfectionism, pessimism, low self-esteem, and a propensity to negative thinking can increase vulnerability to these mean sisters. In addition, circumstantial and environmental factors like stressful and traumatic events, life changes, illnesses, or the loss of a loved one can trigger anxiety or depression.

If you are experiencing depression or anxiety, making it hard for you to function and thrive, overusing social media in a harmful way will make it worse and make it difficult to fully heal and flourish despite receiving professional treatment such as medication and counseling. Yes, it's hard not being on or using social media like everyone else; it's hard not knowing what's going on or feeling like you're missing out. But it's harder to have anxiety. It's harder to have depression. And it's harder to have an eating disorder or other mental health struggle.

You must be willing to do hard things for the sake of your mental health and well-being. You have to be your best advocate and a willing participant in your healing journey. No one can force you to go to counseling, take your medication, exercise, eliminate harmful things in your life, or change the way you think. I know personally how hard it is to fight for your mental health, but it is worth the hard work and sacrifices. Minimally using social media in a positive way protects my mental health, and it's something I'm willing to do to be happy and well (more about this in "After the Reset").

The mean sisters can tend to stick around if we don't get help. If you are having a hard time functioning because of one or both of them, it is important to get professional help because anxiety and depression don't usually get better on their own and often get worse. Professional counseling and medication are two powerful tools we've been given to help us heal. However, they are not the only tools, and there are other ways to improve your well-being. Daily practicing some of the tips I shared in "How to Live Happier and Healthier" and "A Healthy Brain and a Sound Mind" will help you tremendously. I also hope you are finding that your time away from social media is improving your mental health and happiness.

If we're not careful, the mean sisters will convince us we're victims when we're actually more than conquerors through Christ who loves us (see Romans 8:37). They will try to convince us that we are our anxiety, depression, eating disorder, or diagnosis. But we are not a list of symptoms, and our struggle will never be our identity.

You are a dearly loved child of God, and that is the truest thing about you. You don't have to let these mean sisters push you around forever. Anxiety and depression are highly treatable, and with the right care and support, you can experience relief. Through the power of God, renewing your mind, healthy habits, counseling, and professional help when needed, you can thrive and lead a flourishing, wholehearted life.

Reflect

Where is your mental health on a scale of 0 to 10, with 0 being very poor and 10 being excellent?

How does social media impact your mental health? Do you think it is beneficial to use in this season of your life? Are you better with or without it?

What are some steps you can take to improve your mental health?

Pray

God, please heal and protect me from anxiety, depression, and other mental health issues. Give me the support I need, help me to take steps to heal, change my thinking, and empower me to make positive lifestyle changes so I can find freedom and flourish.

Act

What's one brave action you can take today to improve your mental health? You can look back at the practices in "How to Live Happier and Healthier" for ideas.

DAY 25

DEFINING SUCCESS

Success is knowing your purpose in life, growing to reach your maximum potential, and sowing seeds that benefit others.
JOHN MAXWELL

We all want to be successful. The dictionary defines *success* as "the attainment of wealth, favor, or eminence,"[1] which is fame or recognized superiority. Our world portrays success as having wealth, beauty, fame, and impressive accomplishments. Celebrities, influencers, and athletes get gold stars for their beauty, status, and achievements. They are exalted and idolized. Their way of life sparkles and shines. When we compare our lives to theirs, we can seem ordinary.

Today's portrait of success for girls and women can include thousands of social media followers, a designer home with a walk-in closet, gorgeous babies, a booming business, wealth, and the image and body our culture defines as ideal. Many of us are hustling ourselves sick, chasing a life we think will make us happy, but instead, it leaves us feeling empty and disappointed.

Status, fame, beauty, and accomplishments seem to promise ultimate happiness. We are tempted to idolize women on social media who embody this kind of success. We might think that if we attain this false version of success, life will fall into place, and we'll have everything we want. But material things offer false promises and are not everlasting.

As alluring as the world's definition of success is, it is fleeting and superficial. Jesus asked, "For what profit is it to a man if he gains the whole world, and loses his own soul? Or what will a man give in exchange for his soul?" (Matthew 16:26, NKJV). It's meaningless to gain the whole world or achieve social media stardom, fame, status, and wealth at the expense of our relationship with God, well-being, and eternal life.

When we strip away how our culture defines success, we realize that what we really want cannot be found in fame, achievements, or status. More than material possessions or other people's approval, we want emotional well-being and satisfaction with our lives. Zig Ziglar, a renowned motivational speaker, said there are eight basic things people want to feel successful: "Everybody wants the same things—to be happy, to be healthy, to be at least reasonably prosperous, and to be secure. They want friends, peace of mind, good family relationships and hope."[2] These are the essential components of a fulfilling and meaningful life.

> Success is less about what you achieve and more about who you are becoming.

To live a life we're proud of and love, we must define success for ourselves in a God-honoring way. If we don't, other people will define success for us. If we're not careful, people might put their expectations on us. We might try to meet them out of a desire for approval and end up living the way they want us to live, not the life we want for ourselves.

Not everyone will achieve the kind of success that social media and the world praise. Most of us won't be influencers, models, celebrities, or bestselling authors, but each of us can succeed in the things God has put us on this earth to do. The Bible gives us principles that make for a successful and flourishing life. The greatest commandment Jesus taught us is to "'love the Lord your God with all your heart and with all your soul and with all your mind.' This is the first and greatest commandment. And the second is like it: 'Love your neighbor as yourself'" (Matthew 22:37-39).

DEFINING SUCCESS

You can't be successful in God's eyes without loving Him and loving others. This is our greatest purpose. This is true and everlasting success.

Success is less about what you achieve and more about who you are becoming. It's about integrity, character, and who you are in the seen and unseen moments of your life. It's about how you treat others and your impact on this world. The Book of Wisdom teaches us that our reputation is a marker of true success: "A good name is more desirable than great riches; to be esteemed is better than silver or gold" (Proverbs 22:1). This is echoed in Ecclesiastes 7:1, which says, "A good reputation is more valuable than costly perfume" (NLT). Your character is far more important than anything you will achieve. The world looks at outward success, but God looks at who you are on the inside.

True success is about living in a way that honors God. He delights in seeing you live into your full potential and maximize your gifts. Charles Stanley said, "Your potential is the sum of all the possibilities that God has for your life."[3] You have a unique calling, gifts, and talents no one else does. Not living on your phone will automatically give you a competitive edge over everyone else who does, making you happier and more successful. If you swap time on your phone for time becoming excellent at your interests, gifts, and talents, you can accomplish incredible things and live to your full potential. Amazing opportunities can come to you that never will if you scroll through life.

What do you want to be great at? In his book *Outliers*, author Malcolm Gladwell presents the ten thousand rule. From his studies of the most accomplished people, he came to the conclusion that it takes ten thousand hours for someone to become elite at a certain craft, whether it's a sport, writing, singing, computer programming, or playing an instrument. This comes out to twenty hours a week for ten years. What if you traded twenty hours a week on social for twenty hours becoming truly great at something you love and are gifted at? Imagine what an incredible life you could lead and the doors that would open for you.

During this journey, as you continue to shut out the voices of others, take all the time you need to think about what a successful life looks like to you. You don't have to comply with the world's standard of success.

This is your life, and you get to decide how you are going to exhaust every sacred day God gives you. What will it take for you to get to the end of your life and be proud of the legacy you've left behind and what you've accomplished? What changes do you need to make to ensure you will live a meaningful life? Get quiet before God and ask Him to give you a vision for your life that will glorify Him. You were made for a flourishing, wholehearted, and spiritually successful life that makes a lasting mark on this world.

Reflect

How do the world's and social media's voices define success?

What is your definition of success?

If you could be elite at one thing, what would it be? How can you make more time to get better at this?

Pray

God, help me to turn away from the world's standards of success and live a life that glorifies and honors You. Shape my definition of success and empower me to live out my values and accomplish my dreams and goals.

Act

Write down your own definition of success on a Post-it and put it somewhere you can look at it regularly.

DAY 26

FREEDOM AND GRIT

*In the long run, we shape our lives and we shape ourselves.
The process never ends until we die. And the choices
we make are ultimately our own responsibility.*
ELEANOR ROOSEVELT, YOU LEARN BY LIVING

I've heard it said that there are two kinds of people in this world: those who put their grocery carts away and those who don't. I know that might have stung if you're the latter, but it's never too late to take the high road and change! I know the cart guy would really appreciate it. The principle here is that there are people who take responsibility for their lives and others who don't. The most empowering but sometimes terrifying reality is that we have freedom and personal agency. God has ultimate control over our lives, and we will experience hardship and trials in this world, but He gives us freedom to decide how to live and what kind of women we will become.

Having free will and personal agency means we have the power to influence and change our behaviors, thoughts, and actions. We are responsible for how we live. We get to choose the big and small decisions we make, the relationships we have, how we spend our time, what we think, the dreams we pursue, and what we value in life. How we respond to the privilege and responsibility of freedom can lead to a destructive, mediocre, or extraordinary life.

FREEDOM AND GRIT

Personal freedom is good news for every area of your life, including your relationship with social media. Too many people are living in submission to their phones instead of to God. Technology can tempt us to live passively, but Scripture warns us of living an idle life: "A little sleep, a little slumber, a little folding of the hands to rest—and poverty will come on you like a thief" (Proverbs 6:10-11).

Social media and phone addiction can overpower and paralyze you from living with purpose and intentionality. Technology can make you a bystander in your life. If you let this happen, you will look back and regret living your life on a screen. You get to decide if you're going to spend your life on your phone or work hard to invest in your gifts and talents to accomplish things you're proud of that will give you a more fulfilling life.

When we mix the power of personal agency with grit or hard work, we can get incredible results. Grit is a steadfast perseverance in God and the strength we have in Him that allows us to do hard things. It is the quality of persistence, tenacity, passion, and determination to reach a goal despite any obstacles. It's the force that enables us to finish college, pay off debt, be a good mother, run a marathon, and overcome poor mental or physical health. It's the key to turning dreams into reality.

Live the kind of life you can't wait to wake up to.

Grit is a hard and high road, but a road worth traveling on. The path can be steep and exhausting and give you blisters, but it leads to breathtaking destinations. Social media is crowded, but the "gritty" road is not. It is lonely. It is not crowded on the track when you're the only one on your team running the extra mile. It is not crowded at the gym at six in the morning. It is not crowded in the library at nine in the evening. It is not crowded behind a computer screen when you write your first book or on the couch early in the morning during your quiet time when everyone else in your family is sleeping. If the crossroads of freedom and grit were easy, everyone would take them. Like the narrow road toward eternal life, few are willing to take the road called Grit that leads to remarkable destinations. But if do, you'll find your best life.

I do want you to know that self-effort and self-help only go so far. God gave us our lives, and ultimately He is the one who gives us the strength to accomplish anything. We can't do it on our own. Friend, you don't need to strive for success or prove your worth. Yes, it's important to take responsibility for our lives, have wisdom, and work hard, but we must remember our worth comes from God alone and not what we accomplish. We should only pursue goals that glorify God, bring us joy, and maximize our gifts. We should not try to accomplish our goals to impress other people. Meditate on Psalm 46:10: "Cease striving and know that I am God" (NASB). Resist the temptation to hustle for your worth.

It's through God's power living inside you, His grace, and your grit that you can make progress toward your dreams. These three things will make you unstoppable. God honors a life of grit that seeks to glorify Him, not yourself: "Commit your work to the LORD, and your plans will be established" (Proverbs 16:3, ESV). Blessing will follow when you take responsibility for your life, seek to honor God, live with wisdom, and work hard. When you live like no one else, you can experience joy like no one else.

God can do immeasurably more than you can ask, dream, or imagine (see Ephesians 3:20). I know you are capable of achieving great things and living your very best life when you live with wisdom, powerfully harness your personal agency for good, and have tenacity and grit. God's strength is made perfect in your weakness, though, and great is His power living inside of you. You can do all things through His strength (see Philippians 4:13). I hope as you continue to quiet the noise of social media and wake up to the gift and wonder of your life, you will be empowered to become the woman you want to be and live the kind of life you can't wait to wake up to.

Reflect

What does having personal agency mean to you?

_____

_____

_____

What are the driving values in your life?

___

___

___

How do you balance resting in God's grace, relying on His strength, and working hard?

___

___

___

Pray

God, thank You for the freedom and personal agency You give me. Help me to steward my life with wisdom, intentionality, grit, and responsibility. Turn my eyes from worthless things and fix my eyes on things of eternal value. I surrender my life to You and commit to glorifying You in all I do, accomplish, and say.

Act

Write down one hard action step that will help you achieve a personal goal. Make a plan to do it, and ask a friend for accountability if needed.

___

___

___

DAY 27

HOW TO REALLY CHANGE YOUR LIFE

Sow a thought, and you reap an act;
Sow an act, and you reap a habit;
Sow a habit, and you reap a character;
Sow a character, and you reap a destiny.

RALPH WALDO EMERSON

What kind of woman do you want to become? What do you want to be like in one year, five years, ten years? While it is our powerful and loving triune God (Father, Son, and Holy Spirit) who ultimately transforms us, we have the freedom and agency to make decisions that will reap a joyful life. We get to co-create with our Creator the kind of life we want to live. But even with the power of personal agency, we must hold our lives loosely before the One who has numbered all our days: "We can make our plans, but the Lord determines our steps" (Proverbs 16:9, NLT).

Your life is guided by your thoughts, beliefs, habits, and goals. They either keep you stuck or allow you to experience breakthroughs and life to the fullest. Negative thoughts, limiting beliefs, bad habits, and a lack of direction can make an unfavorable life. Positive thoughts, self-confidence, good habits, and inspiring goals are the makings of a great life.

We usually have an idea of the direction we want our lives to go and the things we want to accomplish, but sometimes, we don't know how to get there. Be encouraged—you have what it takes to chase your dreams and catch them. The stepping stones to achieving the life you want include having a confident identity, beneficial behaviors, powerful habits, and clear goals.

Having a confident identity comes from believing who God says you are. This will empower you to make life-giving decisions that will lead you in the direction of your goals and dreams. You can't change your life or behavior without changing what you think of yourself. For example, if you want to run a marathon but believe you are lazy, then your habit of running won't stick because you can't modify your behavior without modifying what you believe about yourself. In order to cross that finish line, you must believe you are an athlete and are capable of accomplishing hard things. Only then will you be able to make lasting changes. When you receive and walk in your God-given identity as His child, you make choices and live in a way that reflects this unshakable identity.

As you begin to cultivate a confident identity, you will build habits that allow you to step into your full potential toward the life you hope to have. If you want to know what you will be like in the future, look at your habits. A habit is "a settled disposition or tendency to act in a certain way, especially one acquired by frequent repetition."[1]

> Our lives are transformed one habit at a time.

Our lives are transformed one habit at a time. Habits can be beneficial, neutral, or harmful. They either keep you stuck or move you in a positive direction. Habits are the building blocks upon which we build our lives. Bad habits are rocks built of soft, brittle sandstone. When you build your house on them, they will crumble and fall apart. Good habits are like solid bricks upon which you can build a life you're proud of. Harmful habits make a challenging life. Good habits make a life worth living.

As we make small incremental changes through habits over time, such as limiting our time on social media, the changes are compounded, and we can have huge breakthroughs and get remarkable results that enhance our lives. We must decide who we want to become before we choose to break bad habits and create good ones. James Clear, author of

Atomic Habits, said, "Every action you take is a vote for the type of person you wish to become. No single instance will transform your beliefs, but as the votes build up, so does the evidence of your new identity."[2]

Every small or big decision you make, and every action you take will influence who you become in the future. Are your habits and decisions moving you to your full potential? Do your actions honor God? It is never too late to change. One study indicated that it only takes sixty-six days to create a new habit.[3] I know you are capable of creating new routines that move you toward your full potential because you can do hard things. Just think how far you've come on this journey already and what good habits you are putting in place of social media.

A keystone habit is a practice that has a domino effect and leads to a series of other habits. An example of a keystone habit is having a daily quiet time in the morning, which positively influences the rest of your day, or a practice of daily exercise that gives you momentum to make healthier choices. What keystone habit do you think would transform your life the most if you began doing it? Other beneficial habits will more easily follow and build upon your foundation. Our daily decisions make it possible for us to reach our goals and become the best version of ourselves—women who are fully alive with joy in our hearts.

Like aimlessly scrolling social media, living without intentionality and a clear direction can lead us somewhere we don't want to be. Having a vision for your future will make you excited about your life, give you hope, and inspire you to press through life's difficulties. When we don't have a motivating vision, we don't actualize the gifts and talents we've been given. Proverbs 29:18 says, "Where there is no vision, the people perish" (KJV). What kind of future makes you excited about your life?

Get quiet and think about what you want to accomplish with your life and the legacy you want to leave behind. Set goals that will maximize your gifts and talents, leading you toward a fulfilling life you can't wait to wake up to. I know you can do this. You are full of so much potential and can accomplish extraordinary things with your life. When you have an unshakable identity, make life-giving decisions, cultivate powerful habits, live intentionally, and surrender your life to God, He can do abundantly more than you can ask, dream, or imagine in your life.

Reflect

List some of your good habits.

_____

_____

_____

_____

List some of your bad habits.

_____

_____

_____

_____

What is one habit you want to break?

_____

_____

_____

_____

What can be your keystone habit that will lead to other successes?

_____

_____

_____

Pray

God, I want to live an abundant life that honors You. Help me believe who You say I am, make good decisions, and cultivate habits that move me toward the woman You created me to be. Show me who I could be if I lived to my full potential, and empower me to choose to become my best self.

Act

Commit to doing your keystone habit for five days and reflect on its impact on your life.

DAY 28

WHIMSY, REST, WONDER, AND PLAY

Live in the sunshine, swim the sea, drink the wild air's salubrity.
RALPH WALDO EMERSON, "MERLIN'S SONG"

Our digital world makes our spirits weary. We must regularly escape and find renewal through the practices of whimsy, rest, wonder, and play. As we do, we wake up from our spiritual slumber. Ephesians 5:14 tells us, "Wake up, sleeper, rise from the dead, and Christ will shine on you." We must rise above anything that has been keeping us spiritually asleep, such as distractions and phone addiction. The radiant light of Christ will then shine upon us and revive us to a full and overflowing life. These practices are free remedies that restore our souls.

We must run boldly to the throne of God's grace, believing He can and will restore our souls. When we draw near to Him, He will draw near to us. When we untangle ourselves from the distractions of the world, we are free to run and play in His presence, and our sleepy spirits wake up and become fully alive.

Prioritizing and practicing whimsy, rest, wonder, and play through daydreaming, relaxing, adventuring, surfing, and laughing has transformed my life and revived my spirit, which was once suffocated by darkness and debilitating depression.

To live a life of whimsy is to find delight in dreaming, playing, and imagining. A whimsical life chases enchanting things with childlike wonder. Did you ever daydream as a little girl—let your mind wander and imagine? Did you ever lie down and stretch on an itchy lawn of green grass, watching marshmallow clouds dance along a powder-blue sky?

When was the last time you unhurried your mind, let it meander without restraint, and embraced boredom instead of reaching for your phone? Studies have found that imagining and daydreaming are healing for your brain. Your brain cannot handle constant stimulation, especially from technology. Good brain health requires times of relaxation.[1] Take time throughout your day to allow your mind to rest, be quiet, and daydream. This will improve your mental health and brain health, reducing anxiety. Next time you feel bored, instead of scrolling social media, quiet your distractions and let your mind wander and dream.

> Envelop yourself in the splendor of creation and find rest.

Resting is the most restorative thing we can do for our worn-out souls. A day of rest, called the Sabbath in the Bible, is not just an invitation; it is a divine commandment from God: "Remember the Sabbath day by keeping it holy. Six days you shall labor and do all your work, but the seventh day is a sabbath to the Lord your God" (Exodus 20:8-10). How kind it is of God to tell us to take a day off. He always knows what is best for us. When we rest, we slow down and live in the present moment.

Having a day of rest reduces stress, inflammation, and the risk of heart disease; improves sleep; restores mental energy; improves creativity, focus, memory, and productivity; and can even add years to your life.[2] Your phone also needs a Sabbath. I love putting my phone on time-out on the weekends. Put your phone to rest on your day off so your mind and soul can be restored. Give it a try and see how you feel.

Resting also slows us down and allows us to live in the present. Many of us have "hurry sickness," defined as a "pattern characterized by continual rushing and anxiousness; an overwhelming and continual sense of urgency."[3] Dallas Willard told a man he mentored, "You must ruthlessly eliminate hurry from your life,"[4] believing it to be one of our greatest spiritual enemies.

When Jesus and His disciples walked the dusty streets of Israel, the pace of life was three miles an hour. Jesus lived in the moment and was never hurried. We can't love people well when we're in a hurry. Jesus invites us to a more peaceful and joyful life. God offers us an escape from the world's stressful and frantic way of life, but it's an invitation only we can accept.

My favorite weekends consist of less than ten phone pickups and wild outdoor adventures! Wild and beautiful places take our breath away. The wonder of creation is a refuge from this world. It leaves us in awe of the God who made it all. Creation calms our minds, soothes our souls, and improves our mental health. When we walk by the sea, scale a mountain and soak in the view, or watch a sunrise or sunset, we see the majesty of God. We remember how small we are and how great God is. We marvel at His works and are moved by the way He romances us through the beauty of what He has made. However often you can, run to the wild corners of the earth. Have dazzling discoveries and exhilarating adventures. Envelop yourself in the splendor of creation and find rest.

John 1:3 says, "Through him all things were made; without him nothing was made that has been made." But even with the miracle of life, not everyone believes. Psalm 14:1 tells us, "The fool says in his heart, 'There is no God.'" Creation gives evidence that there is a Creator, that this all didn't just happen. "For since the creation of the world God's invisible qualities—his eternal power and divine nature—have been clearly seen, being understood from what has been made, so that people are without excuse" (Romans 1:20).

God has made Himself known through creation, and we have no excuse not to believe. Where can you go to soak in the majesty of all God has made? What beautiful places take your breath away and draw you closer to Him? Escape to them as often as you can and let God restore you.

As a little girl, how did you like to play? Kids play tag, kick soccer balls, do cartwheels, run, jump rope, and hang on the monkey bars, laughing as they do. But when we grow up, many of us stop playing, laugh less, and lead sedentary lives. God wants to see us laugh and play with delight. God created us to have fun, run, play, and giggle even as adult women, like we did as children.

Laughter is a medicine you should take every day. Studies have found that laughter strengthens your immune system, boosts your mood, soothes tension, relieves stress, relieves pain, and increases your personal satisfaction in life.[5] Surround yourself with people and things that make you laugh and find fun in moving your body.

Practice whimsy, rest, wonder, and play. Let God breathe His life into your weary soul. You will live freely and lightly as you make these practices a regular part of your life. God gives you these gifts to restore your soul. Receive them and find rest and renewal.

Reflect

Is rest a weekly rhythm in your life? If not, how can you make it a priority and take a day off from work and your phone?

What makes you laugh and play?

Where is your favorite place to marvel at creation, and how can you spend more time in nature?

Pray

God, thank You that because of what You have done for me and all You have given me, I am free to run and play. Help me to find delight in all You made. Help me to laugh and play often, accept Your gift of rest, and marvel at the wonder of all You have made.

Act

List one way for each that you can practice whimsy, rest, wonder, and play. Implement one a day for a week and see how you feel.

Whimsy

_____
_____

Rest

_____
_____

Wonder

_____
_____

Play

_____
_____

DAY 29

A GLORIOUS ADVENTURE

*If you spend yourselves in behalf of the hungry and satisfy
the needs of the oppressed, then your light will rise in the
darkness, and your night will become like the noonday.*

ISAIAH 58:10

There is a difference between being a social media influencer and a woman of influence. Being a woman of influence is about making a lasting impact on the lives of others and the world around you. It's not about generating a lot of attention or persuading people to buy things or dress and live a certain way. It's about influencing people with God's love and helping them know their worth. It's about living on mission for a cause greater than yourself. It's about living a life of depth and integrity that makes others feel loved, seen, and known.

There can be times in our lives, such as seasons of debilitating depression or tragedy, when we barely make it through a day—when it is impossible to look beyond ourselves. In these seasons, we can be still and let God fight for us. But as He heals us and restores our souls, we also heal by looking outward more than inward. Sometimes, the more inward-focused we are, the more unwell we are. Serving others heals our insecurity, shame, and sadness.

Life gets really good the moment we decide to love and help others. That's when joy and freedom begin to steep in our souls. It's when life gets exciting. There is a glorious adventure awaiting women who make the countercultural decision to live beyond themselves and the patterns of this world. As we live for something bigger, we discover the joy and purpose we were created for.

We all have the same purpose in life but different callings, which blend together. Our purpose is to love God, be loved by Him, love others, and enjoy the gift of our lives along with every good and perfect gift from above. We are called to go in joy and gladness to tell others about God's love and the good news for their souls: that forgiveness and eternal life are a gift through faith. Jesus told us, "Love the Lord your God with all your heart and with all your soul and with all your mind. This is the first and greatest commandment. And the second is like it: 'Love your neighbor as yourself'" (Matthew 22:37-39). This is what we've been created to do.

While this is our collective purpose, you have been designed with a unique calling on your life that no one else but you can fulfill. Frederick Buechner said, "The place God calls you to is the place where your deep gladness and the world's deep hunger meet."[1] The world is starving with deep hunger—dark and empty places where justice and mercy are urgently needed. Micah 6:8 says, "He has shown you, O mortal, what is good. And what does the Lord require of you? To act justly and to love mercy and to walk humbly with your God."

You have been made for a glorious adventure, a passionate purpose.

There are lonely grocery store shoppers who need gracious clerks to bag their items and wish them a good day. There are nursing home patients who need loving caretakers to tend to their needs and listen to their stories. There are children from broken homes who need a mentor or family, addicts who need sponsors, impoverished communities that need food and clean water, and people who need a friend.

There are deep needs everywhere, but we must look up to see them—we can't look stiff-necked at our phones. We live in a state of spiritual slumber when we look inward too much or compare our lives to others. We come alive when we look upward to God and outward to people. This is a secret that will change your life. The world will try to tell you that you have to look how she looks and have what she has to be happy. But the secret to joy is basking so deeply in the love of God that you can't help but overflow with it and share it with others. Joy is about taking that love and light and scattering it everywhere your feet take you. Living for ourselves is empty and unfulfilling; living for God is a wild and glorious adventure.

What needs and causes tug at your heart? What makes you want to jump in to make things better? Where do your "deep gladness" and the "world's deep hunger" meet? Reflect on your passions and the ways you find joy in serving. The answers to these questions will be a cue to your calling. You might think your job needs to be your calling or your calling needs to be your job, but you can fulfill your calling and purpose wherever you are, with whatever you have and whatever you do.

Our world needs us to walk in our immeasurable worth and purpose, doing hard and holy things. Think about the lives we could save and the injustices we could overcome if we came together and made it our mission to bring the Kingdom of God to this earth. Imagine what we can do as an army of women if we turn our eyes away from our phones and look for the deep hungers of the world, doing everything we can to feed them. Looking at others' lives on a screen will leave us empty, envious, and insecure. But when we look to God and meet the needs of the world in gladness, we become alive and free.

You have been made for so much more than the life our culture and social media offer. You have been made for a glorious adventure, a passionate purpose. You've been made for a full and overflowing life that makes a lasting mark on the people you encounter. What is God calling you to do with your life? Are you ready to pursue it?

Reflect

What cause are you most passionate about?

_____
_____
_____

Where do you think your gladness meets the deep needs of the world?

_____
_____
_____

When you get to the end of your life, what do you want your legacy to be?

_____
_____
_____

Pray

God, help me to turn away from the trivial things of this world and turn my eyes and heart outward to meet the needs of others. Show me my calling and empower me to make a lasting impact on this world. I give You my life.

Act

Do one act of service this week for someone in need.

DAY 30

LIVE FULLY, WHOLLY ALIVE

*Because your love is better than life, my lips will
glorify you. I will praise you as long as I live.*

PSALM 63:3-4

I predict that one of the greatest regrets many of us will have at the end of our lives is how much time we spent on our phones. William B. Irvine warned us of the danger of "misliving." He said, "There is a danger that you will mislive—that despite all your activity, despite all the pleasant diversions you might have enjoyed while alive, you will end up living a bad life. There is, in other words, a danger that when you are on your deathbed, you will look back and realize that you wasted your one chance at living."[1]

What will it take for you to get to the end of your life and say that you did all you could do with the time God gave you? When you take your final breath, you will have to give an account of how you spent your life. Will you squander it in pursuit of vanities, or will you exhaust every borrowed breath God gave you in a way that makes a lasting mark on the world and the lives of others? Every second of your life—your one and only precious life—is sacred.

With Jesus, who gives us the gift of eternal life, no matter what valleys we walk through in this life, our future is bright. But in order to walk into the promise of this hope and future, we must leave some things behind. We must forget the distractions of this world. We must fix our eyes ahead on the better things of God. As we endeavor toward the good gifts God has for us, we will find the joy, connection, and peace we've been craving. We will find the abundant life our souls have been searching for, and we'll never want to look back.

God is doing a new thing in your life. He will be faithful to complete this good work He started in you (see Philippians 1:6). His goodness and love will follow you all the days of your life as you keep company with Him (see Psalm 23:6). God delights in you. He rejoices over you with singing (see Zephaniah 3:17). You are His masterpiece, His workmanship, wholly and dearly loved. You were created to play an irreplaceable role in God's epic story. A story that ends in victory. You make this world more beautiful by bringing hope and light when you live fully alive by abiding in the radical love of Christ.

Every second of your life—your one and only precious life—is sacred.

It's been an honor to journey with you these past thirty days. As our time together comes to a close, I hope you have recovered your life or maybe even discovered it for the first time. I hope this has been the reset your soul needed. I hope that as you have turned the volume of life down, you have begun to hear the loving whisper of God inviting you to a better life spent in the company of His presence.

I know I've given you some tough love and a lot of things to think about. I've labored and prayed over each of the forty thousand words I have written just for you because I want you to know how sacred your life is and see you live it to the fullest without any regrets. I want you to know how smart and full of potential you are and that you make the world more beautiful because you are here.

As we end our time together, I want to remind you that your value will never be measured by the number of likes, shares, or followers you accumulate. You have been created for a life of joy, purpose, connection, and greatness that this world and social media will try to keep you from.

Your best life will never be found on your phone. I hope you've realized how much agency you have over how you choose to spend your time. By stepping away from the constant noise of social media, I hope you have rediscovered the beauty of solitude, the delight of genuine connection, and the power of presence. I hope you have reclaimed your joy.

This is not the end but a new beginning. Don't let the distractions of this world keep you from your best life. You might think social media is free, but every hour you spend on it costs you something. The cost of seconds, minutes, hours, and years on social media is time you could have spent doing something more meaningful and life-giving. Ultimately, it's a life better lived.

As we close, I want to invite you to pray a prayer that has transformed my life and can transform yours as well. Pray this with bold faith: "God, thank You for Your love and the gift of my life. I ask that You do immeasurably more than I can ask, dream, or imagine in my life through Your power and for Your glory." Pray this with a sincere heart and wait and watch what God will do in your life. You are needed in this world.

God is inviting you to live wide awake to the gift of your life. Don't miss your one chance at living. Live fully, wholly, fearlessly alive. Live courageously, counterculturally, without regrets. Guard your heart and mind. Inhale and exhale your precious breaths with wisdom. Love without abandon. Chase your dreams and catch them. Fight for joy. Walk in your worth. Live loved by God, make God's love known, and when you breathe your last breath, you will be proud of the life you lived and the legacy you'll leave behind.

Reflect

What has this thirty-day journey been like for you?

_____

_____

_____

What do you want to take from it?

___

How do you want your life to be different from here on out?

___

Pray

God, thank You for the gift of my life. Help me live in a way that makes You proud. As I finish this social media reset, please give me wisdom and help me be intentional with every breath You give me.

Act

Fill in the blanks for the following sentence to help you articulate your life passions and mission:

My passion and mission in life is to _____ because I care about _____. I can do this by _____.

After the Reset

Thank you for taking this journey with me. I hope you know how brave and hardworking you are. I hope this has been a life-changing experience that has brought you closer to God, the life you want to build, and the woman you want to become. As you reenter the digital world, do so with intentionality and wisdom. Be encouraged—you have control over what role social media and your phone will have in your life. You can make lasting changes that will safeguard your mental health and set you up for your best life.

You don't have to go back to the unhealthy relationship with social media you might have had before you took this journey. You can make permanent changes that will improve your life. If you want to return to social media, you can decide whether to use it in a positive or negative, helpful or harmful way. You can use it to be a light to other people in a way that adds value to your life.

When I started my journey of cultivating a healthier relationship with social media, I felt trapped. I didn't like what social media was doing to me, but I didn't want to get rid of it completely. I finally found one boundary that changed everything for me and helped me overcome my addiction, which is to not have any social media apps on my phone. Instead, I keep them on my iPad and have time limits.

I can now go days, weeks, or months without using social media and make an effort not to check it on the weekends and in the morning. If I want to share a photo or moment, I never do it in real time but post it hours or days after I capture it on my phone, which syncs with my iPad. This helps me live in the present. Even though comparison can be hard to avoid, I don't follow accounts that make me feel like my life is not good enough, and I also avoid looking at the Search & Explore section. Instead, I follow uplifting and educational accounts and those of friends. And a lot of golden retriever videos! I am so much happier and feel free from the mental distress I used to experience after wasting hours of my life scrolling.

You, too, have an amazing opportunity before you to live wide awake to your one and only life. You don't need to feel stuck endlessly scrolling through other people's experiences. You don't have to use social media like everyone else. You don't have to feel anxious, depressed, or insecure about yourself because of social media. You have permission to live like no one else so you can have joy like no one else. If you still want social media to be a part of your life, you can use it wisely in ways that mostly add value to your life within the boundaries you set with it. You can see the wonder of this world and live fully in the moment. You can have real, meaningful relationships and experience deep soul rest. My friend, you can live this way today! You don't have to wait. Are you ready for a better life?

On page 151, I list several activities you can do instead of being on social media. I then share a quiz to help you understand the impact social media is having on you. There is also an optional mathematical formula you can complete to determine how many days and even how many years you are on track to spend on social media the rest of your life, given your average daily usage. That section is followed by ideas for setting social media boundaries and a space to create your own boundaries.

Then, I share some additional powerful life-coaching questions I encourage you to answer and reflect on whenever you wish. Next, I have a well-being questionnaire you can take however many times you'd like to get a sense of how you are doing spiritually, mentally, and physically. After that, I include a collection of verses written in a letter format called "Father's Love Letter" to help you better understand God's love for you. Lastly, I share a guided prayer you can say to surrender your life to Jesus and be transformed forever.

Now that you've completed your thirty-day social media reset, set aside a time of prayer and reflection to process your journey and all you have learned. This would be a great time to journal and talk with any friends who took the journey with you. Know that this doesn't have to be a one-time experience. You can continue your break from social media even after these thirty days, or you can come back to this book and do another thirty-day reset anytime you feel your soul needs it. Thanks again for allowing me the honor of taking this journey alongside you, and I pray God guides and protects you and makes His face shine upon you.

Love,

Allie

You can connect with me at Alliemariesmith.com.

APPENDIX 1

75 Things You Can Do Instead of Scrolling on Social Media

Here's a list of 75 positive, life-giving things you can do offline to restore your soul; improve your mental, spiritual, and emotional well-being; and enhance your relationships:

1. Ditch your phone for a day and go on an adventure.
2. Lie on the ground and watch clouds dance across a baby-blue sky.
3. Walk barefoot on the grass and look for ladybugs.
4. Read a book under a tree, but don't forget your bug spray.
5. Have a picnic in the park and pack lots of cheese and chocolate.
6. Memorize a Bible verse that helps you overcome anxiety and fear.
7. Grab your journal and list everything you are grateful for.
8. Volunteer for a cause you care about.
9. Move your body with joy and freedom.
10. Take a polar bear plunge into a lake or the sea.
11. Cook a nourishing meal that makes your mouth water.
12. Visit an art gallery to inspire you to make space for creativity.
13. Take a deep breath, fill your lungs with air, and say a prayer of gratitude as you exhale.

14. Sing your heart out at a concert, even if you're tone-deaf.
15. Write a letter to a friend or family member to say you love them.
16. Create a vision board to inspire you.
17. Do something unexpected and kind for a stranger or someone you love.
18. Make something with your hands.
19. Wake up to a sunrise and then catch the sunset.
20. Attend a retreat to reset your life and get closer to God.
21. Plant a garden and get dirt under your fingernails.
22. Go for a bike ride and feel the wild wind in your hair.
23. Get a pet if you have the time and resources to care for one.
24. Take a hot bath with salts and lots of bubbles.
25. Learn to play a musical instrument.
26. Go to counseling.
27. Take your camera and photograph all the pretty things you see.
28. Plan a weekend getaway and drive along the back roads with the windows down.
29. Host a game night with friends.
30. Write ten truth declarations about who God says you are.
31. Hang out with that friend who makes you laugh so hard you could pee your pants.
32. Join a small group or Bible study.
33. Take a dance class and let your booty move.
34. Go to your local farmers' market and buy yourself and a friend flowers.
35. Write a poem.
36. Sleep outside under a canopy of stars.
37. Learn a country's language and plan a trip there.
38. Create a photo book of happy memories.
39. Fall asleep in a hammock under the shade of trees.
40. Cheer on your favorite team at a sports game while wearing face paint.

41. Get artsy: paint, draw, get glue on your fingers, and make a huge mess.
42. Finally, do that DIY project you've been thinking of.
43. Take a pottery class and get clay all over your hands.
44. Eat a chocolate bar or two, and don't feel bad about it.
45. Write verses on sticky notes and place them in every room of your house.
46. Trek a new hiking trail until you get blisters on your toes.
47. Join a book club.
48. Take a silent retreat and practice solitude.
49. Host a potluck with friends, and don't forget the Tupperware for leftovers.
50. Sing karaoke at the top of your lungs and pretend no one is watching.
51. Plan a camping trip, and don't forget the s'mores.
52. Train for a race.
53. Say something nice to yourself and a friend.
54. Do something nice for yourself and a friend.
55. Bake sourdough bread.
56. Visit a botanical garden and smell every flower.
57. Take a scenic boat ride, but wear a life jacket.
58. Play a new sport, but don't get hurt.
59. Learn to talk to God like you would your best friend.
60. Go to the sea and collect a bucket full of shells and sea glass.
61. Attend a play.
62. Volunteer at a nursing home and ask a resident to share their life story.
63. Watch a classic movie with your friends and eat a lot of buttery popcorn.
64. Run away from the city lights and go somewhere wild and free.
65. Go backpacking, but don't forget the toilet paper.
66. Visit a museum or historical site.
67. Host a themed dinner party.

68. Take a scenic train ride and stare out the window until you fall asleep.
69. Let your mind wander and daydream.
70. Write a letter to your future self and younger self.
71. Write your bucket list and make a plan to do each activity on it.
72. Visit a cemetery and reflect on the legacy you want to leave.
73. Make a playlist of your favorite songs and memorize all the lyrics.
74. List the top five things you value most in life.
75. Set six-month, one-year, and five-year goals.

APPENDIX 2

Social Media Quiz

Answer yes or no to the following questions:

1. Do you spend more time on social media than you want to?
2. Do you feel anxious, agitated, or restless when you can't get on your social media accounts?
3. Do you check your social media accounts first thing in the morning, throughout the day, and before bed?
4. Do you scroll through your social media feeds during work hours and frequently throughout your day?
5. Do you find it more enjoyable to spend time scrolling social media than hanging out with your friends or engaging in other activities?
6. Have you been trying to use social media less but can't seem to do it?
7. Do you feel you must constantly post photos, videos, and updates to your social media accounts?
8. Do you experience negative emotions like sadness, frustration, or jealousy during or after your time on social media?
9. Do you compare yourself to others on social media and feel like it negatively impacts your self-esteem or sense of worth?

10. Do your friends or family express concern about your social media usage and tell you you're on it too much?
11. Do you feel pressure to share every aspect of your life on social media to feel validated or accepted and to keep up with what everyone else is doing and posting?
12. Do you frequently lose track of time while using social media?
13. Do you feel social media makes you less productive or interferes with your daily responsibilities?
14. Do you think about social media often, even when you are not using it?
15. Do you regularly check your social media accounts when you are in the physical presence of other people?

After completing this survey, tally up the "yes" responses to assess what kind of relationship you have with social media. If you answer yes to one of these questions (which is so normal and expected!), it indicates that social media is likely negatively affecting the quality of your life. The more times you answered yes, the more of a harmful effect social media is having on your life and the likelier it is that you may have a social media addiction.

APPENDIX 3

Social Media Formula

You can calculate the total number of days or years you will spend on social media from the age you start using it until age eighty (the average lifespan of a woman) using the following formula.

VARIABLES

A_s: Age at which you started using social media
A_e: Age at which you will stop using social media (or age eighty)
H_d: Average number of hours you spend on social media per day

FORMULA

1. To find the total number of days spent on social media:

$$D_{total} = (A_e - A_s) \times 365 \times (H_d \div 24)$$

Where: D_{total} is the total number of days spent on social media.

2. To find the total number of years spent on social media:

$$Y_{total} = D_{total} \div 365$$

Where: Y_{total} is the total number of years spent on social media.

APPENDIX 4

Ideas for Social Media Boundaries

1. **Set time limits.** Set daily or weekly time limits for your social media use, such as thirty minutes a day.

2. **Set app limits.** Use app timers and limits provided by your phone to control usage (e.g., Screen Time on iOS or Digital Wellbeing on Android).

3. **Take dedicated days or weekends off.** Go twenty-four hours or an entire weekend without social media.

4. **Do extended resets.** Take short or long social media resets as needed. Read this book again.

5. **Unfollow and mute.** Unfollow accounts that don't add value to your life and any people who cause negative emotions such as jealousy or insecurity. Mute people whose content you don't want to see.

6. **Set morning and evening restrictions.** Make your morning or evening social media free. For example, refrain from using it the first hour you wake up and one hour before bed.

7. **Manage your notifications.** Turn off all unnecessary notifications to reduce distraction.

8. **Manage your content.** Restrict the type of content you consume (e.g., only inspiring and educational content). This will make the algorithms fill your feed mostly with this kind of content.

9. **Have accountability.** Share your boundaries and social media goals with people who can hold you accountable.

10. **Have physical boundaries.** Keep your phone out of reach during certain activities, such as working, studying, or having dinner with family or friends.

11. **Use it purposefully.** Instead of using social media mindlessly and aimlessly, engage with it intentionally and with a clear purpose.

12. **Set engagement limits.** Limit the number of posts, messages, or comments you make, such as just a few posts a week.

13. **Take social media apps off your phone.** You can access social media on other devices, such as your computer and tablet, so you are not tempted to check it on your phone throughout the day.

14. **Be intentional with who you follow.** You can choose to only follow and engage strictly with close family and friends and people with whom you have genuine relationships. You do not need to follow celebrities, influencers, or people who trigger feelings of envy.

IDEAS FOR SOCIAL MEDIA BOUNDARIES

15. **Show up to encourage.** Instead of being consumed by presenting yourself in a way that will win you the approval of others, show up to encourage other people. Like their posts, send them encouraging DMs, and leave them positive messages. Use it to build relationships and make others feel loved, seen, and known.

List the social media boundaries you want to implement or write your own.

Describe the kind of relationship (if any) you wish to have with social media.

Write your goal for using social media. What purpose is it for?

Write the name of someone you can share your boundaries with who will keep you accountable.

APPENDIX 5

More Reflection Questions

Below is a list of optional reflection questions that will help you live more intentionally. You can answer some or all of them whenever you wish.

- How is your life without social media different from your life with social media?

- Are you happier with social media or happier without it, or do you feel the same? Explain why.

- What kind of person do you want to become?

- Describe in detail your ideal workday.

- Describe in detail your ideal day off.

- List your top five values.

- Are your current habits leading you in the direction of the life you want to have and the person you want to become?

- What does a fulfilling life look like to you?

- What are the top three goals you want to achieve this year?

- How do you define success for yourself?

- What are your core values, and how do they guide your decisions?

- What activities make you feel most alive and engaged?

- What impact do you want to have on the world?

- What habits do you want to develop, and why?

- How do you take care of yourself? What can you do to improve your well-being?

- List some of your personal boundaries and how you can honor them.

- What are some daily rituals that can keep you connected to God?

- What legacy do you want to leave behind?

- Which people in your life give you energy? Which people take it away?

- Are you achieving your goals? If not, what adjustments or changes do you need to make?

- How can you practice forgiveness, both toward yourself and others?

MORE REFLECTION QUESTIONS

- Are you pursuing your dreams or procrastinating? What do you need to do to move forward?

- Who do you look up to, and what do you admire about them?

- How can you make someone feel loved, seen, and known?

- What are some of your limiting beliefs that are holding you back, and how can you overcome them?

- What qualities are important to you in a friend?

- How do you measure progress toward your goals?

- How do you create and maintain a vision for your future?

APPENDIX 6

Well-Being Assessment Inventory

You can complete this assessment at any time to get an idea of your spiritual, mental, and physical well-being. You can also complete it multiple times.

SPIRITUAL WELL-BEING

1. On a scale of 1 to 5, how strongly do you feel that your life has a sense of purpose?

    1–Not at all
    2–Slightly
    3–Moderately
    4–Very
    5–Extremely

2. How often do you experience a sense of inner peace in your life?

    1–Never
    2–Rarely
    3–Sometimes
    4–Often
    5–Always

3. How connected do you feel to God?

    1–Not at all
    2–Slightly
    3–Moderately
    4–Very
    5–Extremely

4. How often do you engage in faith practices such as attending church, prayer, Bible study, etc.?

    1–Never
    2–Rarely
    3–Sometimes
    4–Often
    5–Always

5. How often do you feel lonely?

    1–Always
    2–Often
    3–Sometimes
    4–Rarely
    5–Never

6. How connected do you feel to other people?

    1–Not at all
    2–Slightly
    3–Moderately
    4–Very
    5–Extremely

WELL-BEING ASSESSMENT INVENTORY

MENTAL WELL-BEING

7. How often do you feel good emotionally?

    1–Never
    2–Rarely
    3–Sometimes
    4–Often
    5–Always

8. How often do you feel stressed?

    1–Always
    2–Often
    3–Sometimes
    4–Rarely
    5–Never

9. How often do you experience mental clarity and focus?

    1–Never
    2–Rarely
    3–Sometimes
    4–Often
    5–Always

10. How often do you have a hopeful and positive outlook on life?

    1–Never
    2–Rarely
    3–Sometimes
    4–Often
    5–Always

11. How often do you experience thoughts of self-harm or suicide?

    1–Always
    2–Often
    3–Sometimes
    4–Rarely
    5–Never

12. How supported do you feel by friends, family, or a social network?

    1–Not at all
    2–Slightly
    3–Moderately
    4–Very
    5–Extremely

PHYSICAL WELL-BEING

13. How often do you engage in physical activity or exercise?

    1–Never
    2–Rarely
    3–Sometimes
    4–Often
    5–Always

14. How would you rate your overall energy levels throughout the day?

    1–Very low
    2–Low
    3–Moderate
    4–High
    5–Very high

WELL-BEING ASSESSMENT INVENTORY

15. How would you rate the quality of your sleep?

    1–Very poor
    2–Poor
    3–Fair
    4–Good
    5–Very good

16. How often do you diet, restrict, binge, or purge?

    1–Always
    2–Often
    3–Sometimes
    4–Rarely
    5–Never

17. How would you rate your overall physical health?

    1–Very poor
    2–Poor
    3–Fair
    4–Good
    5–Very good

18. How often do you feel good about or comfortable in your body?

    1–Never
    2–Rarely
    3–Sometimes
    4–Often
    5–Always

SCORING GUIDE

Each question is scored on a scale from 1 to 5. Add all your scores up. Higher scores indicate better well-being in the respective area.

Spiritual Health: Questions 1-6 (Maximum score: 30)
Mental Health: Questions 7-12 (Maximum score: 30)
Physical Health: Questions 13-18 (Maximum score: 30)

Total Well-Being Score: Add the scores of all sections (Maximum score: 90)

INTERPRETATION

0-30: Low well-being
31-60: Moderate well-being
61-90: High well-being

This assessment can help you identify areas of strength and areas needing improvement in your overall well-being.

APPENDIX 7

Father's Love Letter[1]

I want to leave you with "Father's Love Letter," a compilation of Bible verses from both the Old and New Testaments presented as a love letter from God to you. Each line in "Father's Love Letter" is paraphrased, which means that each Scripture passage's overall message has been summarized into a single phrase to best express its meaning. Read this anytime you need to be reminded of God's love for you.

My Child,

You may not know me, but I know everything about you.
PSALM 139:1

I know when you sit down and when you rise up.
PSALM 139:2

I am familiar with all your ways.
PSALM 139:3

Even the very hairs on your head are numbered.
MATTHEW 10:29-31

SOCIAL MEDIA RESET

For you were made in my image.
GENESIS 1:27

In me you live and move and have your being.
ACTS 17:28

For you are my offspring.
ACTS 17:28

I knew you even before you were conceived.
JEREMIAH 1:4-5

I chose you when I planned creation.
EPHESIANS 1:11-12

You were not a mistake, for all your days are written in my book.
PSALM 139:15-16

I determined the exact time of your birth and where you would live.
ACTS 17:26

You are fearfully and wonderfully made.
PSALM 139:14

I knit you together in your mother's womb.
PSALM 139:13

And brought you forth on the day you were born.
PSALM 71:6

I have been misrepresented by those who don't know me.
JOHN 8:41-44

FATHER'S LOVE LETTER

I am not distant and angry, but am the complete expression of love.
1 JOHN 4:16

And it is my desire to lavish my love on you.
1 JOHN 3:1

Simply because you are my child and I am your Father.
1 JOHN 3:1

I offer you more than your earthly father ever could.
MATTHEW 7:11

For I am the perfect father.
MATTHEW 5:48

Every good gift that you receive comes from my hand.
JAMES 1:17

For I am your provider and I meet all your needs.
MATTHEW 6:31-33

My plan for your future has always been filled with hope.
JEREMIAH 29:11

Because I love you with an everlasting love.
JEREMIAH 31:3

My thoughts toward you are countless as the sand on the seashore.
PSALM 139:17-18

And I rejoice over you with singing.
ZEPHANIAH 3:17

SOCIAL MEDIA RESET

I will never stop doing good to you.
JEREMIAH 32:40

For you are my treasured possession.
EXODUS 19:5

I desire to establish you with all my heart and all my soul.
JEREMIAH 32:41

And I want to show you great and marvelous things.
JEREMIAH 33:3

If you seek me with all your heart, you will find me.
DEUTERONOMY 4:29

Delight in me and I will give you the desires of your heart.
PSALM 37:4

For it is I who gave you those desires.
PHILIPPIANS 2:13

I am able to do more for you than you could possibly imagine.
EPHESIANS 3:20

For I am your greatest encourager.
2 THESSALONIANS 2:16-17

I am also the Father who comforts you in all your troubles.
2 CORINTHIANS 1:3-4

When you are brokenhearted, I am close to you.
PSALM 34:18

FATHER'S LOVE LETTER

As a shepherd carries a lamb, I have carried you close to my heart.
ISAIAH 40:11

One day I will wipe away every tear from your eyes.
REVELATION 21:3-4

And I'll take away all the pain you have suffered on this earth.
REVELATION 21:3-4

I am your Father, and I love you even as I love my son, Jesus.
JOHN 17:23

For in Jesus, my love for you is revealed.
JOHN 17:26

He is the exact representation of my being.
HEBREWS 1:3

He came to demonstrate that I am for you, not against you.
ROMANS 8:31

And to tell you that I am not counting your sins.
2 CORINTHIANS 5:18-19

Jesus died so that you and I could be reconciled.
2 CORINTHIANS 5:18-19

His death was the ultimate expression of my love for you.
1 JOHN 4:10

I gave up everything I loved that I might gain your love.
ROMANS 8:31-32

SOCIAL MEDIA RESET

If you receive the gift of my son Jesus, you receive me.
1 JOHN 2:23

And nothing will ever separate you from my love again.
ROMANS 8:38-39

Come home and I'll throw the biggest party heaven has ever seen.
LUKE 15:7

I have always been Father, and will always be Father.
EPHESIANS 3:14-15

My question is . . . Will you be my child?
JOHN 1:12-13

I am waiting for you.
LUKE 15:11-32

Love, Your Dad.
Almighty God

APPENDIX 8

Prayer to Give Your Life to God

Give God your life, and let Him give you an identity, purpose, and worth that lasts forever. Use this prayer as a guide to surrender your heart and life to Jesus.

> *Dear God,*
> *I need You. Thank You that You love me and came to this world to save me. I confess that I am sometimes guilty of sin or living in a way that separates me from You. I ask that You forgive me and renew my heart and life with Your presence.*
>
> *Jesus, I believe You are Lord, that You conquered death, and that nothing will ever separate me from Your love. I trust in You alone, and I accept Your gift of eternal life. Thank You for calling me Your child. I give You my life.*

If you have prayed this for the first time to give your life to Christ, feel free to sign your name and the date of your decision. Now, share this awesome news with someone.

SIGNATURE _____

DATE _____

Acknowledgments

Thank you, Paul, for your joy and unwavering support of the calling God has placed on my life. Mom and Dad, I am grateful for your unconditional love through every season of my life. To my family and closest friends, thank you for your presence in my life, and I can't imagine it without you.

To our entire Wonderfully Made team and our generous supporters, who make it possible to share the love and hope of Jesus with countless girls and women. To every girl and woman of Wonderfully Made, thank you for being a part of our community and giving me my greatest passion.

Dave, thank you for believing in me and opening amazing doors for my writing career. WTA and Jenaye, thank you for your guidance and support. To Jan, Kaylee, Stephanie, and Claire, thank you for making this book the best it could be. Thank you, Eva, for your stunning cover design. To the entire Tyndale team, thank you for believing in this message and for the honor of being one of your authors.

Notes

INTRODUCTION: IS IT TIME FOR A RESET?
1. Jamie Waters, "Constant Craving: How Digital Media Turned Us All into Dopamine Addicts," *Guardian*, August 22, 2021, https://www.theguardian.com/global/2021/aug/22/how-digital-media-turned-us-all-into-dopamine-addicts-and-what-we-can-do-to-break-the-cycle.
2. Maria Clark, "40+ Frightening Social Media and Mental Health Statistics," Etactics, November 12, 2020, https://etactics.com/blog/social-media-and-mental-health-statistics; Donna A. Ruch et al., "Trends in Suicide among Youth Aged 10 to 19 Years in the United States, 1975 to 2016," *JAMA Network Open* (2019): https://doi.org/10.1001/jamanetworkopen.2019.3886.
3. "Global Social Media Statistics," DataReportal, accessed August 11, 2024, https://datareportal.com/social-media-users.
4. "Social Media Addiction & Usage Statistics," The Grove Estate Addiction Treatment, updated April 25, 2024, https://grovetreatment.com/addiction/statistics/social-media/.
5. "Average Daily Time Spent on Social Media Platforms among Teenagers in the United States in 2023," Statista, accessed September 22, 2024, https://www.statista.com/statistics/1451257/us-teens-hours-spent-social-networks-per-day/#:~:text=Overall%2C%20girls%20spent%20almost%20an,to%204.4%20hours%20for%20boys; Susan Laborde, "Teenage Social Media Usage Statistics in 2023," Tech Report, updated May 30, 2024, https://techreport.com/statistics/software-web/teenage-use-of-social-media-statistics/.
6. Fabio Duarte, "Average Screen Time for Teens (2024)," Exploding Topics, November 10, 2023, https://explodingtopics.com/blog/screen-time-for-teens.

DAY 1: RESTORING YOUR SOUL
1. C. S. Lewis, *The Problem of Pain* (Macmillan, 1947), 139.

DAY 2: YOUR WILD AND PRECIOUS LIFE
1. Mary Oliver, "The Summer Day," in *House of Light* (Beacon Press, 2012).

DAY 3: WONDERFULLY MADE

1. Eva Bianconi et al., "An Estimation of the Number of Cells in the Human Body," *Annals of Human Biology* 40, no. 6 (November–December 2013): 463-471, https://doi.org/10.3109/03014460.2013.807878.
2. Suzana Herculano-Houzel, "The Human Brain in Numbers: A Linearly Scaled-Up Primate Brain," *Frontiers in Human Neuroscience* 3, no. 31 (November 2009): https://doi.org/10.3389/neuro.09.031.2009.
3. "Amazing Heart Facts," Nova Online, accessed September 26, 2024, https://www.pbs.org/wgbh/nova/heart/heartfacts.html; "Heart Facts Infographic," American Heart Association, accessed September 26, 2024, https://newsroom.heart.org/file?fid=59a7145e2cfac2546cae1995.
4. Reena Mukamal, "How Humans See in Color," American Academy of Ophthalmology, June 8, 2017, https://www.aao.org/eye-health/tips-prevention/how-humans-see-in-color#:~:text=The%20visible%20spectrum%20for%20humans%20falls%20between%20ultraviolet,that%20light%20and%20reflects%20the%20rest%20of%20it.
5. John D. Currey, *Bones: Structure and Mechanics* (Princeton University Press, 2002), 3.
6. "Biblical Commentary (Bible Study) Psalm 139," Sermon Writer, accessed September 26, 2024, https://sermonwriter.com/psalm-139-commentary/.

DAY 4: THE TRUEST THING ABOUT YOU

1. Brennan Manning, *Abba's Child: The Cry of the Heart for Intimate Belonging* (NavPress, 2015), 33.
2. Henri J. M. Nouwen, *Life of the Beloved: Spiritual Living in a Secular World* (Crossroad, 2002), 59.

DAY 6: BE THE DECORATOR OF YOUR LIFE

1. John A. Naslund et al., "Social Media and Mental Health: Benefits, Risks, and Opportunities for Research and Practice," *Journal of Technology in Behavioral Science* 5 (April 20, 2020): 245–257, https://doi.org/10.1007/s41347-020-00134-x.

DAY 9: THE STRENGTH OF SOLITUDE AND SILENCE

1. Dallas Willard, *The Spirit of the Disciplines: Understanding How God Changes Lives* (HarperCollins, 1990), 160.
2. Taylor Leamey, "5 Benefits of Solitude and Why You Need It for Your Mental Health," CNet, March 8, 2023, https://www.cnet.com/health/mental/5-benefits-of-solitude-and-why-you-need-it-for-your-mental-health/.
3. Willard, *The Spirit of the Disciplines*, 163.

DAY 10: A HEART AT REST

1. Belle Wong, "Top Social Media Statistics and Trends of 2024," *Forbes*, updated May 18, 2023, https://www.forbes.com/advisor/business/social-media-statistics/.
2. Dave Ramsey, *Total Money Makeover: A Proven Plan for Financial Fitness* (Thomas Nelson, 2013), 29.

NOTES

DAY 11: LOOKING FOR LIKES, LONGING FOR LOVE
1. Jesse Fox et al., "Effects of Taking Selfies on Women's Self-Objectification, Mood, Self-Esteem, and Social Aggression toward Female Peers," *Body Image* 36 (March 2021): 193–200, https://www.sciencedirect.com/science/article/abs/pii/S1740144520304393.

DAY 12: LADY WISDOM AND LADY FOLLY
1. Allie Marie Smith, *Wonderfully Made: Discover the Identity, Love, and Worth You Were Created For* (Moody Publishers, 2021), 147.

DAY 13: A HEALTHY BRAIN AND A SOUND MIND
1. Eric R. Kandel et al., *Principles of Neural Science*, 5th ed. (McGraw-Hill, 2013).
2. David J. Chalmers, *The Conscious Mind: In Search of a Fundamental Theory* (Oxford University Press, 1996).
3. Norman Doidge, *The Brain That Changes Itself: Stories of Personal Triumph from the Frontiers of Brain Science* (Penguin, 2007).
4. Daniel G. Amen, *Change Your Brain, Change Your Life: The Breakthrough Program for Conquering Anxiety, Depression, Obsessiveness, Lack of Focus, Anger, and Memory Problems* (Harmony, 2015), 16.

DAY 14: SHOWING UP AS YOUR TRUE SELF
1. Codependence was first conceptualized by Dr. Karen Horney, in what she called a "moving toward" personality type. See Karen Horney, *Our Inner Conflicts: A Constructive Theory of Neurosis* (Routledge, 2013). It was popularized by Melody Beattie in her 1986 book *Codependent No More: How to Stop Controlling Others and Start Caring for Yourself* (Hazelden, 1986).

DAY 15: YOU ARE NOT AN IMPOSTER
1. Marwa Azab, "Overcoming Imposter Syndrome: 6 Evidence-Based Strategies," *Psychology Today*, August 29, 2023, https://www.psychologytoday.com/us/blog/neuroscience-in-everyday-life/202308/overcoming-imposter-syndrome-6-evidence-based-strategies.

DAY 16: BREAKING UP WITH YOUR IDEAL SELF
1. *Oxford Advanced Learner's Dictionary*, s.v. "ideal (*n.*)," accessed October 6, 2024, https://www.oxfordlearnersdictionaries.com/us/definition/english/ideal_2.
2. *Merriam-Webster Dictionary*, s.v. "ideal (*n.* and *adj.*)," accessed October 6, 2024, https://www.merriam-webster.com/dictionary/ideal.
3. Sanchari Sinha Dutta, "Eating Disorders and Social Media," News Medical and Life Sciences, updated March 28, 2022, https://www.news-medical.net/health/Eating-Disorders-and-Social-Media.aspx.

DAY 19: HEALING FROM SHAME
1. Curt Thompson, *The Soul of Shame: Retelling the Stories We Believe about Ourselves* (InterVarsity Press, 2015), 63.

2. Brennan Manning, *Abba's Child: The Cry of the Heart for Intimate Belonging* (NavPress, 2015), 12.
3. Allie Marie Smith, *Wonderfully Made: Discover the Identity, Love, and Worth You Were Created For* (Moody Publishers, 2021), 86.

DAY 20: FINDING YOUR PEOPLE

1. Christie Hartman, "Loneliness Statistics: By Country, Demographics & More," The Roots of Loneliness Project, updated March 27, 2024, https://www.rootsofloneliness.com/loneliness-statistics.
2. Ryan Jenkins, "3 Things Making Gen Z the Loneliest Generation," *Psychology Today*, August 16, 2022, https://www.psychologytoday.com/us/blog/the-case-connection/202208/3-things-making-gen-z-the-loneliest-generation.
3. *Oxford Advanced Learner's Dictionary*, s.v. "community (*n.*)," accessed October 8, 2024, https://www.oxfordlearnersdictionaries.com/us/definition/english/community?q=community.
4. Branka, "Facebook Statistics—2024," Truelist, updated February 17, 2024, https://truelist.co/blog/facebook-statistics/.
5. Thomas Moore, "What Is the Average Amount of Instagram Followers?" *Viralyft Blog*, updated July 29, 2024, https://viralyft.com/blog/average-amount-of-followers-on-instagram.
6. Moira Lawler, "Is There a 'Right' Number of Friends to Have?," Everyday Health, July 24, 2023, https://www.everydayhealth.com/emotional-health/is-there-a-right-number-of-friends-to-have/.
7. Dale Carnegie, *How to Win Friends and Influence People* (Simon and Schuster, 2009), 56.
8. Rebecca McLaughlin, "Going to Church Could Save Your Life," The Gospel Coalition, May 29, 2020, https://www.thegospelcoalition.org/article/church-save-your-life/.

DAY 21: BEAUTY SECRETS

1. Allie Marie Smith, *Wonderfully Made: Discover the Identity, Love, and Worth You Were Created For* (Moody Publishers, 2021), 61–62.

DAY 22: MAKING PEACE WITH YOUR BODY

1. Jasmine Fardouly et al., "The Mediating Role of Appearance Comparisons in the Relationship between Media Usage and Self-Objectification in Young Women," *Psychology of Women Quarterly* 39, no. 4 (2015): 447–457, https://doi.org/10.1177/0361684315581841.
2. Alana Papageorgiou, Colleen Fisher, and Donna Cross, "'Why Don't I Look like Her?' How Adolescent Girls View Social Media and Its Connection to Body Image," *BMC Women's Health* 22, no. 261 (June 27, 2022), https://bmcwomenshealth.biomedcentral.com/articles/10.1186/s12905-022-01845-4.

DAY 23: HOW TO LIVE HAPPIER AND HEALTHIER

1. Sarah D. Pressman et al., "Association of Enjoyable Leisure Activities with Psychological and Physical Well-Being," *Psychosomatic Medicine* 71, no. 7

NOTES

(September 2009):725–732, https://www.ncbi.nlm.nih.gov/pmc/articles /PMC2863117/.

DAY 24: THE MEAN SISTERS

1. Renee D. Goodwin, "Trends in Anxiety among Adults in the United States, 2008–2018: Rapid Increases among Young Adults," *Journal of Psychiatric Research* 130 (November 2020): 441–446, https://www.sciencedirect.com/science/article /pii/S0022395620309250?via%3Dihub; Qingqing Liu, "Changes in the Global Burden of Depression from 1990 to 2017: Findings from the Global Burden of Disease Study," *Journal of Psychiatric Research* 126 (July 2020): 134–140, https://www.sciencedirect.com/science/article/pii/S0022395619307381 #:~:text=Results,representing%20an%20increase%20of%2049.86%25.
2. Maria Clark, "40+ Frightening Social Media and Mental Health Statistics," Etactics, November 12, 2020, https://etactics.com/blog/social-media-and -mental-health-statistics.
3. Jessica Booth, "Anxiety Statistics and Facts," *Forbes*, updated October 23, 2023, https://www.forbes.com/health/mind/anxiety-statistics/.
4. "Anxiety Disorders," World Health Organization, September 27, 2023, https:// www.who.int/news-room/fact-sheets/detail/anxiety-disorders.
5. "Depressive Disorder (Depression)," World Health Organization, March 31, 2023, https://www.who.int/news-room/fact-sheets/detail/depression.
6. "U.S. Teen Girls Experiencing Increased Sadness and Violence," CDC Newsroom, February 13, 2023, https://www.cdc.gov/media/releases/2023/p0213-yrbs.html.
7. Sean Rossman, "Screen Time Increases Teen Depression, Thoughts of Suicide, Research Suggests," *USA Today*, November 17, 2017, https://www.usatoday .com/story/news/nation-now/2017/11/17/screen-time-increases-teen-depression -thoughts-suicide-research-suggests/874073001/.
8. "'Depression: Let's Talk' Says WHO, As Depression Tops List of Causes of Ill Health," World Health Organization, March 30, 2017, https://www.who.int/news /item/30-03-2017--depression-let-s-talk-says-who-as-depression-tops-list-of-causes -of-ill-health.
9. "Depressive Disorder (Depression)," World Health Organization.

DAY 25: DEFINING SUCCESS

1. *Merriam-Webster Dictionary*, s.v., "success (*n.*)," accessed October 12, 2024, https://www.merriam-webster.com/dictionary/success.
2. Dan Schawbel, "Zig Ziglar's Tips on Becoming Successful in Life," *Forbes*, updated August 19, 2011, https://www.forbes.com/sites/danschawbel/2011 /08/11/zig-ziglars-tips-on-becoming-successful-in-life/.
3. Charles F. Stanley, *How to Reach Your Full Potential for God* (Thomas Nelson, 2009), 201.

DAY 27: HOW TO REALLY CHANGE YOUR LIFE

1. *Oxford English Dictionary*, s.v. "habit, (*n.*)," accessed June 20, 2024, https:// www.oed.com/search/dictionary/?scope=Entries&q=habit&tl=true.
2. James Clear, *Atomic Habits: An Easy & Proven Way to Build Good Habits & Break Bad Ones* (Avery, 2018), 38.

3. James Clear, "How Long Does It Actually Take to Form a New Habit? (Backed by Science)," James Clear (website), accessed June 21, 2024, https://jamesclear.com/new-habit.

DAY 28: WHIMSY, REST, WONDER, AND PLAY
1. Barbara Field, "5 Positive Effects of Daydreaming," Verywell Mind, updated April 9, 2024, https://www.verywellmind.com/positives-about-daydreaming-5119107.
2. Rhett Power, "A Day of Rest: 12 Scientific Reasons It Works," Inc., January 1, 2017, https://www.inc.com/rhett-power/a-day-of-rest-12-scientific-reasons-it-works.html.
3. Rosemary K. M. Sword and Philip Zimbardo, "Hurry Sickness," *Psychology Today*, February 9, 2013, https://www.psychologytoday.com/us/blog/the-time-cure/201302/hurry-sickness.
4. John Mark Comer, *The Ruthless Elimination of Hurry: How to Stay Emotionally Healthy and Spiritually Alive in the Chaos of the Modern World* (WaterBrook, 2019), 19.
5. "Stress Relief from Laughter? It's No Joke," Mayo Clinic, accessed September 22, 2023, https://www.mayoclinic.org/healthy-lifestyle/stress-management/in-depth/stress-relief/art-20044456.

DAY 29: A GLORIOUS ADVENTURE
1. Frederick Buechner, *Wishful Thinking: A Theological ABC* (Harper & Row, 1973), 95.

DAY 30: LIVE FULLY, WHOLLY ALIVE
1. William B. Irvine, *A Guide to the Good Life: The Ancient Art of Stoic Joy* (Oxford University Press, 2008), 1–2.

APPENDIX 7: FATHER'S LOVE LETTER
1. Father's Love Letter used by permission Father Heart Communications ©1999 FathersLoveLetter.com.

About the Author

ALLIE MARIE SMITH is an award-winning author, speaker, podcast host, life coach, and the founder and CEO of Wonderfully Made, a national nonprofit organization dedicated to helping girls and women know their God-given value, identity, and purpose and lead flourishing lives. She started Wonderfully Made at the age of twenty, and since then, it has encouraged millions of girls and women through its events, media content, and resources.

She is the author of *Wonderfully Made: Discover the Identity, Love, and Worth You Were Created For*. Allie has directed dozens of events for over ten thousand young women and the women who love them in California and Hawaii. She has mentored hundreds of young women to help them know their value and believe they can overcome life's challenges.

As a lifelong athlete, Allie is passionate about pursuing a healthy, active lifestyle. She lives in North Santa Barbara County, California, with her husband, Paul, where she loves writing, surfing, playing with horses, and adventuring up and down the coast. Visit her website at Alliemariesmith.com and learn about Wonderfully Made at Wonderfullymade.org.

Tyndale | REFRESH

Think Well. Live Well. Be Well.

Experience the flourishing of your mind, body, and soul with Tyndale Refresh.

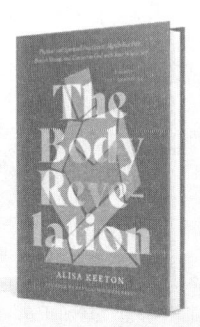

CP1841

WONDERFULLYMADE
KNOW YOUR VALUE

Wonderfully Made is a ministry dedicated to helping you know your God-given value, identity, and purpose and live a flourishing, wholehearted life.

WONDERFULLYMADE.ORG

View our website for resources and encouragement.

Notes